A true story

Fucking hell, this is the last thing I expected …
… I don't know what we're gonna do …
… he's alive!!!

ISBN 978-1-909455-61-0 (Paperback)

Cataloguing-In-Publication Data.
A catalogue record for this book can be obtained from the British Library.

Copyright © 2024 Lasse Spang Olsen. All intellectual property and associated rights are hereby asserted and reserved by the author in full compliance with UK, European and international law. No part of this book may be copied, reproduced, stored in any retrieval system or transmitted in any form or by any means, including in hard copy or via the internet, without the prior written permission of the publishers to whom all such rights have been assigned worldwide. The moral right of the author to be identified as author of this work is hereby asserted in accordance with the Copyright, Designs and Patents Act, 1998.

All photographs and illustrations are the copyright of the author (subject to the same conditions above) except where stated otherwise, or where attempts to ascertain copyright were unsuccessful.

Cover Design © 2024 Dived Up.

Published 2024 by

Dived Up Publications
Bournemouth • United Kingdom
Email info@divedup.com
Web DivedUp.com

The Diver and the Cook

Trapped in 102 Feet of Water

Lasse Spang Olsen

To the crew of *Jascon 4*

Contents

Dedication   *5*
Publisher's note   *8*
About the author   *9*
Preface   *11*

1	The Toilet Was Now on the Ceiling, and I Was on the Floor	*13*
2	From Rusty Pipes to a Hearse	*29*
3	They Eat the Eyes, Ears and Nose First…	*39*
4	We Are Expecting to Find a Body Here	*41*
5	Treading on a Mattress or a Body Feels Just the Same	*67*
6	Grace, Grace, Grace	*79*
7	What the Fuck??	*83*
8	I Have No Idea What to Do	*89*
9	How the Hell Do We Get Him Out	*101*
10	The Plan	*111*
11	The Cook Always Survives	*119*
12	Three Went Down, Four Came Up	*141*
13	On Land Again … and Into the Water … Again	*149*
14	Dancing Makes You Happy	*157*

Postscript: The Open Hatch   *161*

How We Did It   *165*

Acknowledgements   *170*

Index   *171*

Publisher's note

The views and opinions in this book are those of the author and not necessarily shared by the publisher. The text is based on the author's knowledge, experience and expertise concerning which the publisher cannot accept responsibility. Readers should draw their own conclusions concerning the possibility of alternative views, accounts, descriptions or explanations.

The images in this book were taken during the actual rescue, as well as in reconstructions created by the author and his team, and during interviews. Where necessary, they have been restored and/or edited, although they remain true to the subjects and situations they were taken in.

About the author

Veteran filmmaker Lasse Spang Olsen boasts a forty-plus year career. He has participated in stunts and effects in over six hundred films, directed eleven features, and filmed extensively underwater. He's led expeditions uncovering historical mysteries like the *Flying Enterprise* wreck and documented adventures worldwide. He's also a producer, lecturer and author. *The Diver and the Cook* was first published in Danish as *Dykkeren of Kokken* (Feb 2024).

Preface

The events in this book really happened, even though some of what I will describe sounds impossible. I first heard this story right after the events occurred. I was working with some commercial divers on Gibraltar, and they told me a crazy tale about a guy they knew very well. About a shipwreck, an almost impossible rescue mission, bad luck, good luck, incredibly brave divers, and an improbably happy ending against all odds.

I thought it was such an amazing story it should be on TV, and I tried to find the parties involved. But at that point the account started to unravel. It had not, after all, happened to someone that my diver co-workers knew *that* well. But they did know him. A bit.

I had been told that the events happened in the Mediterranean, but that turned out to be wrong. About seven thousand kilometres wrong. It all sounded too unlikely to be true and since no-one really knew the parties involved, I finally decided that it had to be another one of the many misleading stories in the diving business. They often build on a small foundation of truth that is told over and over until it becomes a Salvador Dalí-esque fairytale of monumental proportions — and the slim foundation of truth disappears beneath the exaggerated details. I started to work on other things and eventually forgot about it.

Several years later I was making a documentary for national television in Denmark about some of the world's most extreme divers and the story popped back into my head. What if it *was* true…? Or if even some of it was… And we quickly re-located the parties involved. It turned out that back then, an international offshore company had effectively shut down those parties — forbidding them to talk about what had happened. Since then, the company had not only been bought by someone else but had also collapsed and disappeared — and the people involved were no longer bound by confidentiality. Now we could make contact with them.

In particular, I can thank offshore manager Tony Walker for making it possible to tell this story today. His enormous help and knowledge of all the details of the rescue operation, in which he actively participated, has been invaluable. It's only because of his help that it was possible to get in touch with those involved and to gain access to the many hours of video and audio recordings from the entire incomprehensible event.

All of which means I can tell accurately the story of what happened in the wrecking and recovery of bodies from the tugboat *Jascon 4* at the end of May 2013. I've spent more than three years researching the facts and interviewing the people that experienced them.

So, when I write what they were *thinking, saying,* or *feeling,* it's based on their own actual statements. Sometimes the characters in the story speak for themselves through direct quotes, and sometimes I quote from the authentic radio communication they had during the event. This is thanks to the entire rescue mission being recorded in both sound and video by the divers' helmet cameras. The only changes I have made are in the interests of making the narrative flow. The images with timecodes are from the video recorded during the actual events. When I write about or attribute quotes to either the 'control room' or 'dive control,' this is for simplicity because in reality there were several different people fulfilling that role, all working together.

The following is exactly what happened at the end of May 2013.

Lasse Spang Olsen

1

The Toilet Was Now on the Ceiling, and I Was on the Floor

The stove was a large, old-fashioned galley range that took quite a long time to get hot enough to prepare breakfast. So, the first thing that ship's cook, Harrison, did when he was woken by his alarm clock at a little past four in the morning was turn on the sizable burners, before going into the shared bathroom on the deck where his cabin was located, to brush his teeth.

The ship was tossing from side to side as usual in a way that would have seemed worrying, or at least very uncomfortable, to normal people, but to the crew of the tugboat it was just an ordinary day.

Jascon 4 was a 31.5-metre-long tugboat with a twelve man crew, in a fleet of a hundred offshore ships of different kinds and sizes, all part of the oil industry in the eastern Atlantic off the coast of Nigeria. The tug's job was to tow large international oil tankers to and from *oil barges*. A *barge* is a kind of enormous flat-bottomed boat situated far out at sea above the oil fields. Here the oil is sucked up from beneath the ocean floor and used as both fuel and cargo for the huge tankers.

Jascon 4 was built to cope with almost any kind of weather, so even though the ship was being battered by huge waves, an almost constant thing this far out at sea, there was no real danger at this point. All the crew had to do was hold tight to the railings or door handles as they moved around the ship.

From eight o'clock the night before, *Jascon 4* had been towing a large tanker to the oil pumps on a barge and making sure it stayed put while loading the oil. Now, at about four in the morning, the oil tanker had slacked the wire tethering it to *Jascon 4*, so that the two ships could separate.

Harrison entered the shared bathroom lined with two large sinks, industrial washing machines and dryers along one wall, and toilet booths along the other. Four sailors from the first shift that morning were already there, brushing their teeth, so Harrison decided to first attend to his necessaries until there was more room for him to clean his own teeth.

The four sailors knew each other well. All of them — Harrison too — had been aboard the tugboat for a long time. The crew were a tightly knit and cheerful team.

While Harrison was using one of the toilet booths, a particularly large wave tipped the tugboat and made the ship heave over. One of the men out by the sinks shouted to Harrison in the booth that the ship was sinking. Harrison laughed and responded with a joke. The ship continued heaving.

'At what point did you realize something unusual was going on?' I asked Harrison during our first interview.

'When I was in the toilet booth, I was joking with the men brushing their teeth and suddenly I heard the bosun shout: "We are sinking, we are sinking!"' He told me, and continued, 'but because it is a tugboat, and we are always thrown about in the sea I just figured he was joking. But a moment later we tipped violently to the left — and then to the right. And then we flipped over.

'It was all so fast... before I could even get a hold of the handle of the door, we had turned upside down. And I smashed directly into the door, hit the handle on the way and fell down. The toilet was now on the ceiling, and I was on the floor — the floor, that just a moment ago had been the ceiling. The next thing I saw was the toilet that fell down. "Boah!" It hit me in the head, and I was bleeding. But I did not care about the wound — all I thought of was how to get out of the booth because now the door was stuck.'

There was an atmosphere of confusion and even though Harrison was dazed by the blow he had taken to the head from the heavy toilet, he realized he had to get out of the now upturned toilet booth. But when he tried to open the door — now upside down — he couldn't. He was trapped. During his fall he had ripped off the door handle and now the door was irrevocably shut.

In a state of panic, he looked around the small toilet booth.

The thirty-one-metre-long ship was now lying upside-down far out to sea. Harrison was well aware that something was seriously wrong.

The tugboat *Jascon 4* capsizes.

The ship's cook, Harrison Okene.

The men in the adjacent room shouted for help and Harrison realized that the top of the toilet door (which was now at the bottom) had a ventilation grid. He managed to wrench a piece of metal out of the grid and with it to pry the door open. Then he emerged into the chaos that just a few minutes earlier had been the shared bathroom. The massive industrial washing machines had fallen onto the floor and hit the men that had been brushing their teeth. One lay lifeless under one of the huge machines while the other two screamed at Harrison to free them from where they lay trapped under the wreckage.

At that moment all the lights went out and the inside of the ship went pitch-black.

'I never knew what was going on. Everything went dark. Blackout. It had all gone so fast when the vessel turned upside down. I had only one clear thought in that moment: "We are dying."

'The bosun tried to help the guys out from underneath the heavy washing machines. One of the guys who was trapped said to me, "Give me your hand, give me your hand."

'We tried to get him out, but we couldn't. He had been badly injured by the heavy machines that had fallen on him.'

Harrison looked around for help and heard some of the crewmen shouting out in the passageway. At the end of the passageway outside the bathroom, was a door leading to the outside deck of the ship. Three crew members were trying to open the door to get out to the lifeboats.

'Everyone was panicking,' Harrison continued, 'and they cried out saying we were sinking. But at this point there was no water inside the vessel. We had turned upside down, but there was no water ... yet.'

The sight of the passageway and the door was at once both completely normal and completely unreal. It looked as it always did, except that all the NO SMOKING and EXIT signs looked strange ... they were all upside down. The ship was floating the opposite way to how it should ... it was bottom up and top down ... or at least, that's how it looked to the people inside. But that was a false impression because it was not floating any more. However, since they were not aware of that, Harrison ran towards the men by the door to follow them out of the ship. But the door to their escape was locked.

In Nigerian waters, every outside door on the ship was locked at six o'clock every night. That part of the sea is heavily infested with pirates and the only doors allowed open at night were the two to the bridge, where the chief officer and the captain had of necessity to be able to get outside and orientate themselves. From the bridge they had a clear view of the sea around, could spot pirates in time to get to safety and lock the doors before an attack.

By that point, because the ship was upside down, the two unlocked doors on the bridge were located two floors below the locked door that Harrison and the sailors were trying to open.

An outer door on a ship like this is really two doors — one outside the other. The inner one is made of metal with a strong lock, and the outer is a so-called 'watertight door' made of solid steel and locked with four or six handles to keep all water out and resist the breaking waves that sometimes burst up over the ship's rail.

Both these doors were now blocking Harrison and the other sailors from getting out on deck. What they were unaware of was that the door would not have led them out onto the deck and to the lifeboats. Had they actually managed to open the door, it would have led directly into the Atlantic Ocean. The ship had already been underwater for some time, making its way toward the seabed, keel upward.

Then, the water started rushing in.

'We could not get out. We did not understand what was happening. We could just feel the vessel sinking. Then the water started coming … from below. It leaked in and started covering our legs.

'We still worked on the door because we knew that if we didn't get out right now, we were going down with the ship.'

At first, no-one really reacted to the water surging in and covering their feet — feet which were now standing on what had just been the ceiling. They kept frantically trying to break open the door. Then suddenly things started to move fast. With a thundering racket of noise all the air was pressed out of the ship as water started flooding unhindered into the ship from all sides.

'I saw the water coming from below and I was struggling to stand. It occurred to me that if I stayed in the same place as these guys, trying to open the door, then I was going to drown. Let me just swim further inside the ship. I never even knew where I was headed to, I just knew I had to get out of there.'

The ship was flooded in a matter of minutes.

Harrison fled for his life. Or tried to. For the flooding water made it impossible to run. It was already up to his waist as he tried to escape. Instinctively he left the door and moved further inside the dark ship — the worst direction to head in a ship that's rapidly sinking.

'I was struggling to stand and the sound of the water was so loud. There was so much water all at once. It came from all sides with a massive force. BAM! It caught us and pushed us.'

The flooding water sent bunks, mattresses, shoes, clothes, tables and chairs spinning around. Refrigerators and machines were thrown about with massive force and bowled the crew members over as the ship was filled by the heavy influx. There were sounds of tearing metal, doors breaking off, air being pressed out through narrow passageways and stairwells, furniture being crushed and men desperately crying out as the ship filled up.

'The space was not wide enough for me to swim, so I just tried grabbing on, to hold the walls and push myself away from the water. I pulled at anything and everything I could get a hold of and pushed myself as far away from the water as I could. Further and further into the ship.'

Suddenly, Harrison felt the water lift him up and press him forward. One of his crewmates grabbed onto Harrison's foot and tried to pull himself to safety. He pulled Harrison under the roaring water and Harrison had to kick himself free. The man had to let go and was swept into a cabin by the water. Harrison was carried away down the passageway, further into the sinking ship.

'The water pushed me into the second engineer's cabin with great force. I was struggling but I couldn't fight against it. The force of the water was so strong.

'When it pushed me into the tiny cabin, I thought, "I'm going to die."'

The cabin Harrison ended up in was at the very end of a passageway that was a dead end, on the far side of the deck. He was almost as far into the ship as it was possible to go, with no means of escape. The water was deafening as it filled the rest of the space inside the ship, while men cried for help in the cabins and rooms around him.

'I heard the vessel's mast being crushed and I felt some kind of landing as the ship stopped moving… That's when I realized: we were on the seabed. The ship had completely sunk.

'My first thought was that we were dying. It was all I could think, really: We are going to die!

'When the vessel hit the seabed this fear, you see, it was all-consuming inside of me. "This vessel is on the seabed. How are we going to get out of this place?" There was just this immense fear in me.'

The flood of water receded, and the heavy ship settled on the ocean floor. A deafening silence replaced the roaring waters. Now there was only the wailing sound of the large shipwreck, slowly sinking into the mud of the seabed, mixed with sounds of splashes as the water settled inside the flooded cabins.

But not every cabin had been completely flooded. Not yet.

'The water didn't rise so fast anymore,' Harrison continued, 'although I was sure that it would slowly — but for sure — close in around me very soon. So, I tried to call for help. "Help, help, help, help!" From somewhere else inside the ship, I could hear other men shouting… just shouting, shouting, shouting — everyone was shouting.'

Harrison prepared himself to drown. He thought of his wife and his mother and closed his eyes. But he didn't drown and, after a while, opened his eyes again.

'I looked around the cabin. It seemed like the water had stopped rising.

I could still keep my head above water. And I could see. Strangely, it wasn't dark even though all the electric lights had gone out.'

Harrison could see in the previously pitch-black cabin. And strangely, the water had stopped rising. The small cabin was filled with water up to about a metre from the ceiling. The ship was slightly tilted, so only the upper part of the cabin was above water. Harrison had ended up in an air pocket. Carefully, he looked around the small space above the water. Illumination came and went — in flashes.

'There was some kind of light. Blinking, blinking. And I saw two life jackets, but the buoyancy in them had been damaged by the diesel oil from the engine room that came into contact with them — so they didn't float anymore. But the emergency light worked. That's where the light came from. It blinked … so I could see a little.'

Harrison had found a life jacket with an emergency light.

The emergency lights on the life jackets had been activated when they came into contact with the water. The flickering illumination gave Harrison a temporary opportunity to orientate himself in the small space where he had ended up. The cabin was, of course, upside down. Any loose items were now floating on the surface — only things which were bolted down were not. The room was about three square metres, and only the corner was above water — with about one metre to the ceiling, which had previously been the floor. The water reached Harrison's chest. He knew water would likely eventually penetrate the cabin, and his only chance was to somehow find a way out. As long as the small emergency light blinked on the life jacket, he would be able to see a little, which was essential because it was a long way to the nearest exit. He would hardly be able to find his way in the dark, and those small emergency lights don't shine for very long, so he was in a hurry.

'I thought that with the light, maybe I could see underwater and find a way out of the ship.'

But the only exit on this deck was the watertight door he had tried before. The door was down a long passageway, reached by passing a small area with several doors leading to other cabins, directly outside the cabin Harrison had ended up in. But now, everything was submerged in the pitch-black interior of the ship.

'Fear filled everything inside me at that moment, and the thought of dying was there all the time. But the next thing I thought was, "Let me see if I can get out."'

Harrison grabbed the blinking emergency light and dived. He quickly realized that it was a long swim underwater to the door that lead to the outer deck. Besides, there was virtually no visibility in the murky water. On a regular day Harrison knew the ship's layout by heart, but now it was pitch dark — in water with zero visibility — filled with floating furniture he might crash into or get tangled in, and everything he knew had been turned 180 degrees. Left was right, up was down.

'At that time, I thought that maybe someone had managed to open the door to the deck and get out, so the door was open. It was a long swim, and it was difficult to find the right way. Several times, I was close to swimming through the wrong door and getting lost inside the dark wreck. I swam underwater, and I felt like I was about to explode... I could hardly hold my breath. When I finally reached the watertight door leading to the deck, I saw that the door was still closed. I couldn't hold my breath anymore and was almost suffocated, so I had to fight my way back to get air, and as I swam back, I was again close to getting lost.'

Disheartened, Harrison eventually made it back to the small cabin. It was a long time to hold his breath, and the water was cold. He was aware, of course, that if he continued like this, he would get lost and wouldn't be able to find his way back to the air pocket which gave him, at least for a while, the chance to breathe.

Few people have experienced swimming inside a narrow shipwreck. The movies you see of divers in wrecks don't look much like this did. Because here, there was *nothing* to look at. There was complete darkness, and even when the small lamp on the life jacket blinked, it was designed to *be seen*, not to function as a flashlight. It wasn't much use for finding your way.

Normally, when people try diving while holding their breath, they know that if they really need air, they can just surface again and breathe. It wasn't like that here. There was no 'up' for Harrison. Also, the ship was still filled with furniture, equipment and people's belongings, all floating in a twisted mess in the water. Some things were heavy and lay like great obstacles under the water. Some were lighter, making it easier to bump into them. Or they might move and pose a new obstacle that wasn't there earlier, which you would not want to encounter on the way back to the air pocket. Others could be sharp or get tangled in your clothes.

Despite this, Harrison still had only one plan — to try to swim underwater to the door and get out. He still had no idea that the *Jascon 4* was thirty-four metres underwater and that the journey out through the flooded ship and up to the surface would undoubtedly have cost him his life.

He would never have been able to hold his breath for so long, and if against all odds he had, there would be no rescue. The Atlantic Ocean is very big — it's a long swim inland when you are thirty-nine kilometres from shore. But he would never have had to face this problem, because his lungs would have burst before he even reached the surface. That's because that far underwater everything is under immense pressure. The deeper you go, the more everything is compressed. Even the air inside you. The air Harrison filled his lungs with inside the air pocket would expand as he swam up towards the surface. By the time he got there it would have expanded to more than four times the volume it was down on the wreck and there is no room for that much air in the lungs.

At a depth of thirty-four metres, the body doesn't float and you are almost weightless ... there is virtually no buoyancy. So, you have to really work at it and swim upward to reach the surface before you run out of breath. But as you get closer to it, something happens — the body begins to gain natural buoyancy in the water, partly due to all the air in the lungs which makes them very effective flotation devices.

Suddenly, things start to go very fast — you really gain speed — and the narrow windpipe, which is trying to let all the air out of the lungs, simply cannot empty them quickly enough to keep pace. Then the lungs burst. Harrison would be dead before he reached the surface. But he didn't know this. His only thought was to get out through the door to the upper deck.

'I checked the cabin to see if I could find something I could use. I found some straps and some tarps. I tore them apart and made a rope, so I could tie a line around my arm, allowing me to find my way back to the air pocket in the cabin.'

Harrison made a fifteen-metre-long lifeline. He tied one end to the cabin and held the other end in his hand, took a deep breath, and dived. He swam through the flooded corridors to the exit door and tried to force it open. When he couldn't hold his breath any longer he retreated as quickly as he could back to the air pocket, using the tied strap. Again and again he tried to get out.

'I had no idea how deep the wreck was. I only thought about how to get out. When I was underwater trying to open the watertight door to the deck, I felt something floating above me. I assumed it was part of all the furniture floating around, and I grabbed it to use for stabilization. But when I grabbed it, it felt strange. I took a closer look and discovered that it was a human body. And it dawned on me that the others on the ship ... my friends ... were dead.'

Harrison was inside a wreck, submerged in the Atlantic Ocean. He was trapped behind a double steel door, locked from the outside. There was absolutely no way he could escape alive. His shipmate was lying lifeless in the water, pressed up against the ceiling above the door, along with shoes, clothes and random items floating around the ship. He was most likely not the only one of Harrison's eleven shipmates who had already drowned in the surging black water. Harrison was sure that it would be his turn soon if he didn't find a way out of the wreck. And it was pretty hard to be optimistic about that.

'The moment I felt the dead body in the corridor, I got really scared.

Because I realized that I had to work faster to get out. Otherwise, I would also die, and the wreck would most likely soon be completely filled with water, so my small air pocket would disappear. So, I kept thinking constantly about how to get out. I had already tried the only exit, and it was hopelessly locked, and there was nothing I could do. I had to swim back with the help of my homemade lifeline just to be able to breathe in the small air pocket … and then swim back to the door and my friend's dead body to try to open the door again … and again.'

After many attempts, Harrison had to admit that the door was impossible to open, and if he kept trying, the lack of air and the chilling effect of the cold water would take his life, just as it had most of his shipmates. But when he got back to the nearly flooded cabin, he found to his surprise — and joy — that he was not the only survivor. Faintly, he could hear other voices desperately calling for help from various places in the ship.

'I heard the cries from some of the other crew members, who apparently also had air somewhere in the wreck. "Help, help!" At first, I was glad to discover that I wasn't the only one alive. They shouted, shouted, shouted, shouted. And I thought that maybe I could find my way to them, and we could try to get out together. It made me happy and gave a little hope.'

Harrison tried to find other ways around the ship. Perhaps only a short dive was needed to reach one of the other air pockets where a comrade was trapped. But the more he tried, the more he understood that there was no way out of his underwater prison. There was no way to help his desperate crew mates.

'After some time, the voices slowly faded. First one … then one more … and then another. I couldn't help them. I could hear them die one by one, and I couldn't do anything.'

All Harrison could do was sit and listen to the desperate cries for help grow more and more hoarse. He felt a profound sense of helplessness.

'It made me feel really bad when I could hear my colleagues die because I was like a mother to them on board the vessel. I cooked, and we always lived like a family. They came to me, one after the other, they told me their stories, challenges, marriage problems, life stories. So, when I saw these guys with families, children, big, big dreams … when they disappeared here in the cold water in the darkness at the bottom of the sea, I lost all hope because drowning in the dark is the worst way to die. I was very sad for my friends in that moment.'

Harrison had to accept that he was trapped in the wreck and would die there. One by one, the shouting sailors' air pockets were either swallowed by the sea or the oxygen in them was used up. Eventually, most of the cries stopped, and Harrison had long given up trying to go to their aid. He had to stay in his own small air pocket, left to himself in the dark wreck.

'There was one person who held on … he kept shouting for help. It was the cadet trainee, the youngest on board. But there was no way I could help him. I wished we had been two in the cabin I was in. He shouted and shouted for help for a long time — and then … I didn't hear his voice anymore. So, his … that was the last voice I heard. I kept shouting for help. Help … help! But no-one answered.'

Then Harrison sat there — alone, hungry, and thirsty, but with enough air not to die right away.

'I only thought about how to get out. But at the same time, of course, I was hungry. I saw a bag inside a cabinet, I saw a can of Sprite and a Coke. And I saw a sardine can in the bag.

'I opened the coke, and I opened the sardines, and I was pinching the sardines into my mouth and drank a little of the coke, so I had something in my tummy. Just a bit of Coke and a bit of sardine.'

Although Harrison knew that this cramped cabin would be where he would die when the oxygen in the air pocket ran out or the water slowly squeezed out the air, his survival instinct told him he couldn't just keep standing up to his chest in water. The water off the coast of Nigeria is warm. Even at thirty-four metres deep where he was, the water temperature was around twenty-seven degrees. Warm enough to survive for a long time. But Harrison had already been there for a long time. He was freezing and needed to have as much of his body out of the water as possible.

There was not much life left in the small flashing emergency beacon on the life jacket. The light was gradually becoming a weak little blink.

Authentic photo of Harrison inside the shipwreck.

'I noticed the cabinets hanging on the wall in the cabin. I pulled out what was in the cabinets and managed to break them off the wall, creating a pile of them along with the furniture in the cabin. Anything I could find that could be used to make a small raft... The walls of the cabins are covered with a kind of fibre, and I pulled it off and used it... I took one of the cabinet doors and placed it on top so I had something to sit on, so I could keep as much of me above the water as possible. It was not possible to get completely out of the water, so my legs and my stomach were still submerged.'

Harrison managed to gather the furniture and equipment floating on the surface into a pile up against one wall so that he could pull his body as far out of the water as possible.

Slowly, the battery on the blinking light in the life jacket that had allowed him to see just a bit inside the small flooded cabin faded away. Darkness took over completely.

'When the light from the life jacket went out, the whole place became pitch-black again. I had no light. No light at all. But I wasn't really scared because I had experienced blackouts many times in my life, so I was just there. In the dark.'

In Nigeria, where Harrison grew up, it's not uncommon for the electricity supply to be interrupted. Most houses have a diesel generator, but often they don't work, or people can't afford the fuel. So, Harrison was used to darkness and had spent many evenings and nights in complete darkness. But now, as he sat utterly alone inside the sunken ship, he was surprised at how dark darkness can be. No darkness in his life had been so dark before. There was nothing to see. Not a single reflection. Nothing was distinguishable from anything else. Everything was completely, uniformly black.

After a while, he became desperate. Not so much because of the darkness, but because everything seemed just as hopeless as the darkness that surrounded him.

'I cracked. I started trying to smash the ship. I beat it with whatever I could find in the cabin, fire extinguisher, furniture … anything … I slammed it against the wall because if I could just break it, I could get out. But it didn't happen. The walls of a ship are very solid. But I kept hitting and hitting to break them and make a hole. I wished it would just happen. But, of course, it did not, so I just sat down in the end. And I realized … "I'm trapped" … And the only thing going through my head was, "If I die, will I just die like this? No one knows where I am, you can't find my dead body, I can't call anyone, I can't even talk to anyone. I will leave my wife, my family, my mother …" We had just lost two of my sisters, so my mother was really, really down and crying a lot … "and if this happens to me, if I die … I don't know if she will be able to hold herself up, or if she will take her own life." That was the feeling I had at that moment, and I started crying. I was there alone in the dark … just sitting. The little I could see was when I sneezed … then I saw some kind of stars … small lights behind my eyelids … inside my head. So I tried to sneeze … it gave a little light inside me. They were the only lights I had.'

A long career as a ship's cook in the offshore industry had taught Harrison that the only hope for rescue would be from divers. But since divers are often part of the crew on offshore ships, Harrison knew enough about diving to be fully aware that no diver in Nigeria would be able to save him from a shipwreck like this.

In the Nigerian diving industry, they almost always dive on air, with regular scuba tanks on their backs, and it would be entirely unthinkable for such divers to penetrate a shipwreck at the bottom of the sea. They would never have enough air in their tanks for such an operation.

Harrison was deep inside the wreck — almost as far as one could get from an exit. It would take any diver a very long time to get all the way in. The chance that anyone would take such a risk was close to zero. That was a fact.

He resigned himself to dying in there.

2

From Rusty Pipes to a Hearse

Tony Walker was heading up to the control room on the commercial diving vessel *Lewek Toucan*. A big ship in diving terms, at eighty metres long by twenty metres wide, it was equipped with a large helipad and all the most modern offshore equipment.

Tony entered the control room, where four other men were already present. Colby Werrett, an experienced diving supervisor, was sitting at the desk, overseeing the divers on assignment. The others were coordinating the divers' air supply, the ship's position and technically monitoring the ongoing tasks.

The large diving vessel *Lewek Toucan*.

The divers they were monitoring were in the process of laying a pipeline on the seabed well off the coast of Nigeria. Tony Walker, who had just started his morning shift, was the offshore manager for the task. That meant he was the liaison between the customer and the diving vessel, responsible for ensuring the task was completed and that any issues were addressed in the best way possible. He had just received a call from the diving vessel's office on shore. They had been contacted by one of the many independent companies operating off the coast of Nigeria. There was a very specific reason they had been contacted. *Lewek Toucan* was not a regular diving ship but something rather unusual in those waters … a 'saturation' vessel which carried so-called saturation (or sat) divers.

Sat divers are able to work under pressurized conditions at deep sea levels for an extended period of time. On board the diving vessel, the divers enter a compression chamber where they stay for twenty-eight days. The chamber pressure is slowly adjusted until its interior, where the divers live, matches the pressure at the depth they are going to work at. They are still on board, but inside the chamber at a completely different pressure to the rest of the ship. The divers cannot leave the pressurized chamber or open it to the outside during those twenty-eight days. The chamber is their home for the duration. Their only private space consists of a narrow bunk and there is not much room inside.

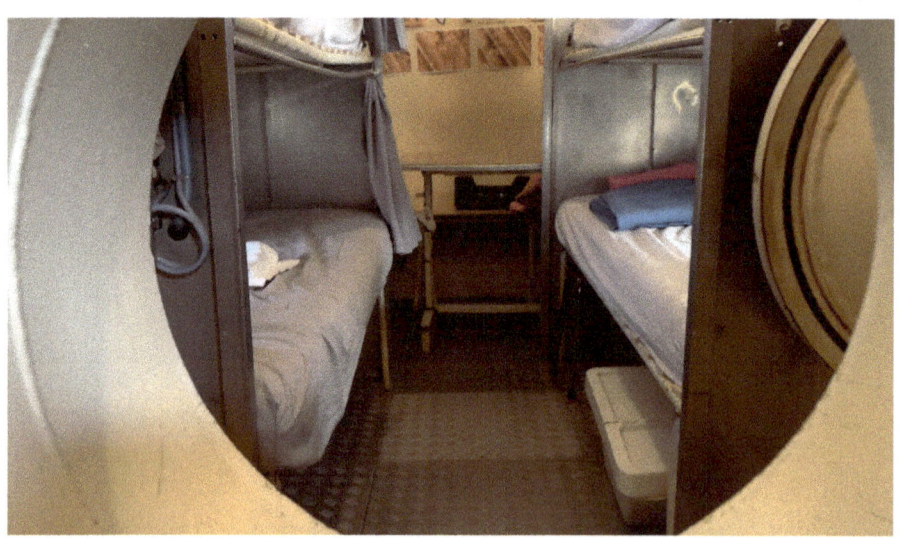

Sleeping quarters for four people in a compression chamber. Your privacy is your bunk.

Saturation divers at work.

These kinds of divers usually don't swim. They mostly walk around on the seabed, so their diving suits are different to those of other divers. They wear large metal diving helmets which are sealed tightly to their suits. On the helmets are powerful spotlights and cameras that allow a control room up on the ship to see what the divers see. Thus, they can direct divers' actions via radio communication inside their helmets.

When the divers have to dive, they leave their living quarters in the compression tank and open a solid round hatch that sits vertically like a door but closes with a turning handle, resembling one you might find in a submarine. They crawl into an adjacent, very small chamber called a 'bell.' The bell is not integrated with the rest of the pressure chamber system and can be detached and lowered to the sea beneath the ship.

Inside *Lewek Toucan*'s diving bell. This photograph was taken with a wide-angle lens — in reality, there is even less space than there appears to be in this image.

Because the divers have already been living in — and will return to — the compression tank on the ship, all the time remaining under the same pressure as the depth they are diving, unlike regular divers they do not need to spend time decompressing when they finish their dives.

Decompressing involves slowly ascending — with prescribed stops at specific depths — depending on how long and how deep one has dived. If you ascend without decompressing, there will be a lot of excess nitrogen in the body and it can cause decompression sickness, also known as 'the bends.' It is life-threatening, so anyone who dives must make a very slow ascent with pauses at the right places to avoid injuries. Regular divers, who dive from — and back up to — the normal surface pressure (the pressure we all walk around in every day), usually spend time decompressing every time they come up. This means they cannot dive for very long at any one time, as they need enough air to breathe all through the dive and as they decompress on the way up. The deeper you dive, the longer the decompression takes. Sometimes divers hang in the water for hours after each dive.

'Regular' divers with scuba tanks, in the process of decompressing.

But *saturation* diving, where divers are pressurized in a chamber on the ship, is an ingenious solution for larger tasks on the seabed. Sat divers can dive for as long as they need to. They only need to think about decompression when they are ready to leave the pressurized tank after their twenty-eight-day shift. In theory, there is no limit to how deep sat divers can go and how long they can dive at a time. Usually, it is said that sat divers can go down to three hundred metres, but in theory they can go deeper if the ship has a long enough cable in the bell.

A sat diver and their thick umbilical cable.

Sat diving ships with pressure chambers and diving bells are not typically found in the part of the world where Harrison's tugboat sank. It's an extremely expensive way to dive, and there aren't any such local ships. It was an unusual occurrence that there was a large foreign diving ship with sat divers in Nigerian waters when the *Jascon 4* sank.

The tugboat's owner contacted the sat diving ship to ask if they could be released and sail to the accident site. It would take the large diving ship at least a day to reach the wreck of the tugboat. But speed was not important. The task the owner of the wrecked tugboat had contacted the *Lewek Toucan* about involved recovering the bodies of drowned sailors, so there was no hurry.

Such a task could not be carried out by 'ordinary' divers, which the offshore industry in Nigeria had plenty of. It would be both dangerous and inadvisable to send ordinary divers into a wreck with many floors, lots of passageways, cabins and stairs, at that depth.

That was the task which offshore manager Tony Walker was on his way to present to the divers and crew. Tony had no idea how it would be received, being asked to retrieve dead sailors from a shipwreck was definitely *not* something they were accustomed to.

'When did you first hear about *Jascon 4* and the sinking?' I asked Tony.

'Early morning on May 26, we were called to a meeting with the diving team and the crew on board, where we were asked if we could help another offshore company with something. One of their tugboats had sunk overnight with all hands-on deck, and they wanted to know if there was any possibility that we could go and retrieve the bodies from the wreck using our sat equipment.'

Sat divers are underwater craftsmen. They weld, build and move things. They recover equipment from the seabed and cast foundations. In general, they do all sorts of things underwater, but none of the things they do, or are trained for, comes close to recovering dead people.

I asked the diver Nico Van Heerden how he felt about possibly having to search for dead people.

'I'd never done anything like that before. But they asked us if anyone would prefer not to do it. I mean, we were contracted to weld oil pipes underwater, not to recover bodies. So, it was a pretty daunting prospect to get ready for.'

Tony explained, 'I talked to everyone who would be involved because I knew what might happen … that we would find dead bodies. And we gave everyone the option not to dive if they didn't want to. But all to a man they said that they would dive. Nobody had any reservations at all.'

Nico elaborated: 'I sat there in the compression chamber with nine other big brawny divers. If everyone says "Yes," then you're gonna say yes as well. I wouldn't want to be the only person who said "No." So … there was a bit of peer pressure — but ultimately, if you were one of the people that drowned in that vessel that sank, you would also want your body to be found so your family could bury you. Even though I had no desire to find dead people, it's just something you have to do in that situation. I would wish that someone else would do it for me, and most people probably felt the same, so we agreed that — even though it was an unpleasant task — it was something we should do. There was complete agreement to help. Or, at least, no-one wanted to be the one to say no.'

'We were quite a distance away,' Tony said. 'So, there would be about twenty-two hours of transportation time from where we were to the wreck of the sunken ship.'

The *Lewek Toucan* began the slow process of rigging down what they were doing and setting course for the wreck of the tugboat *Jascon 4*.

Offshore manager Tony Walker at the entrance to a recompression chamber.

Diving ship *Lewek Toucan*.

3

They Eat the Eyes, Ears and Nose First...

It was night again. Not that that had any significance for Harrison, at the bottom of the inverted wreck on the seabed. It had been darker than the darkest night for a long time. But the fact it was night again meant he had now spent a full day inside that tiny claustrophobic space, with water up to his waist. Breathing had become a struggle. The air felt thick, it tasted bad. There was not much oxygen left in it.

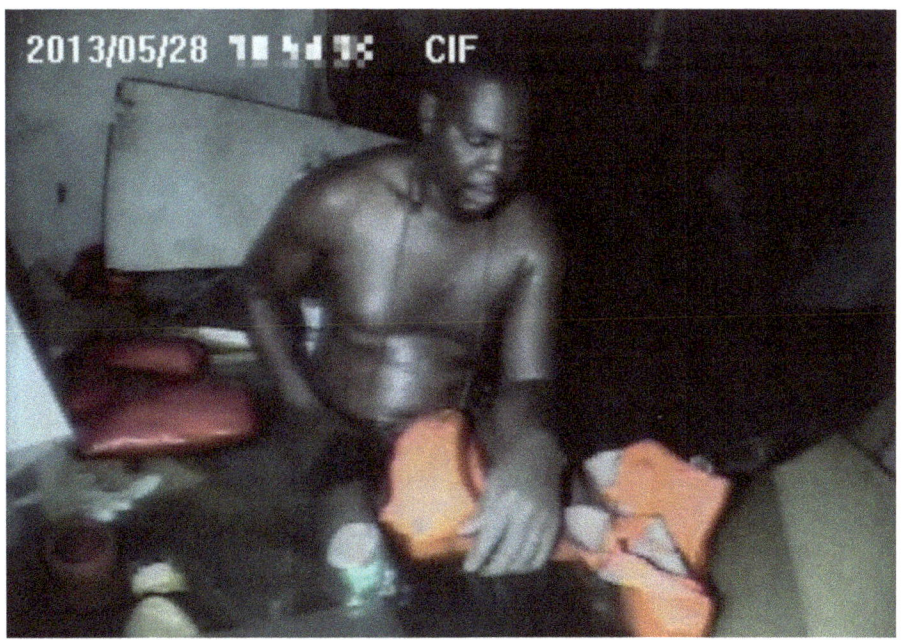

Authentic picture of Harrison trapped deep inside the ship.

But Harrison's troubles didn't end there. Even though he had built a small 'island' from the cabin's furnishings to raise himself up as much as possible, he had been partly immersed in the cool seawater for twenty-four hours. New problems were slowly emerging.

'Suddenly, I started to feel it... like a mosquito biting you. It's the same feeling. They bite you. So, I knew "That is crayfish... and crabs." I remembered that when someone falls into the water and ends up on the seabed, that's when the crayfish and crabs come. They go for the ears, the eyes, the nose. They probably assumed I was already dead, so they were trying to eat me. They bit me all over my body, everything that was in the water. It suddenly overwhelmed me with a massive fear... it reminded me quite literally that I would soon die, and these animals would devour me. I couldn't stop them because my feet and legs were in the water. I felt the animals eating me... they bit, bit, bit... and I just felt pain and bites all over my body. Nothing else.'

As if that wasn't enough... fate decided to turn it up a notch. Harrison heard something close to him in the pitch-black water.

'I became really scared when I heard something biting... like an animal trying to chew something. It bites like this, CHOW, CHOW in the water... I thought, "Is this a shark or a barracuda?" Those were the two things that came to my mind. I believed that the door to the deck and the sea might have opened, that predators had found their way in, and now they were eating the dead bodies of my friends. I try to keep an eye on my feet and legs, which were still underwater, but there was nothing I could do because everything was so dark. So, I tried to feel if the water bubbled or if I could sense any movement in the water, so I could try to kick the animal or something. I was really scared because I knew I was going to die, and... to be eaten by these animals at the same time. There's nothing I could do to stop it... so I just tried to survive. Then I started praying and I said, "God, if it is your will that I die like this, then it's not a problem. If I know it's your decision. But if it's not your will, find a way out for me so I can get out of this place. If it ends here, let it end. But God, if it is your will, as it is in Heaven, I'm ready to die now."'

4

We Are Expecting to Find a Body Here

Two and a half days after *Jascon 4* had sunk and — as far as anyone knew — without a single survivor, the eighty-metre-long diving ship, *Lewek Toucan* arrived at the site. There was no hurry, since the bodies to be found and recovered had already been lying on the seabed for two days and were likely to remain where they were.

The first dive team of three men prepared to be lowered down to the wreck. One man would dive into the wreck and search for bodies. The second would be a support diver, always staying outside the wreck to assist with managing the umbilical for the diver who was alone inside. An umbilical is a bundle of tubes and cables which supplies a diver with air, light, communication and heat. The final man in the trio would stay in the diving bell and monitor the instruments.

The diver who would go inside the wreck was Nico. I asked him if he could remember how he felt at that time.

'I'll never forget that. I sat in the bell and went through the notes and technical drawings of the shipwreck, trying to memorize them so I had a chance to navigate inside the upturned ship. I tried to guess how the dive would unfold... I was quite stressed at the thought, as we normally never dive into wrecks, and I was honestly afraid of getting lost in there or getting stuck... and I had absolutely no desire to handle the dead sailors I had to go in and look for.'

The divers were lowered the thirty-four metres down to the wreck, which lay upside down on the seabed, with the stern buried in mud and the bow slightly higher. The wreck had sunk so deep into the mud that the top part of the wheelhouse was also buried, and one of the first challenges would be to find a place where Nico could enter the ship.

Sat divers usually don't swim; they walk out of the diving bell which has transported them down to the seabed. Bells are bell-shaped, somewhat resembling heavy duty glass bottle recycling banks, and are not much bigger. They are full of instruments and equipment, and when the three people they are built to transport are all inside, there is little extra space. If you suffer from claustrophobia, you shouldn't become a sat diver.

Each dive team consists of three divers: one in the diving bell and two outside: diver 1 and diver 2. Diver 1 performs the tasks. Diver 2 is primarily a safety diver, helping diver 1. The three divers rotate with each new dive, but throughout the entire dive the roles remain unchanged.

This time, it was the turn of South African diver Nicolaas (Nico) van Heerden to be diver 1 and, therefore he was the one who had to perform the primary task: going inside the perilous wreck.

'This was actually only my second dive after I graduated as a sat diver. I was the least experienced, so ... in that team, I was basically the baby. But the way it works in a three-person diving bell team is that you rotate and change roles in the group every day, and that day it just so happened that I was diver 1. And that's why I was the one who had to dive into the wreck. There was nothing to be done about it.'

Sat diver Nico van Heerden.

Tony Walker explained: 'That day, Nico was diver 1, and all the time he was inside the wreck, he was completely alone. No one could go in with him.'

Nico elaborated: 'I think all the other divers thought, "It's great, it's not me who has to go into the wreck ... it's perfectly fine that Nico has to go in first."'

Many thoughts went through Nico's mind while the diving bell slowly transported the three divers down to the wreck. Since it was only Nico's second saturation dive, he did not have the same experience with the equipment as the others. As far as he knew, no sat divers had previously penetrated a shipwreck at that depth. The equipment is cumbersome and takes up a lot of space, so it would most likely be extremely challenging to move around inside a tugboat like the one waiting for him on the seabed. Most ships, especially those not carrying passengers, are surprisingly cramped. Stairwells, door openings, cabins and corridors are built as small and narrow as possible to optimize space on board. It would undoubtedly be difficult to move around.

Nico is a large and quite broad-shouldered guy. With the large diver's helmet and extra gas tank on his back, he would take up almost twice the space of an average slim person. As a sat diver, he would also be pulling a heavy diving hose behind him, meaning he would be pretty immobile and could easily become stuck. The further he entered into the wreck, the more dangerous it would become, as it would grow increasingly difficult for the safety diver outside the wreck to help. At the same time, the likelihood of getting stuck would rise, as the air hose would have to be pulled around more and more corners. And, naturally, the longer it had to be pulled — the heavier it would become. The more Nico wondered whether it was fair that he was the one to take the first eight-hour shift inside the wreck, the more he started to think that it might have been a bad idea to agree to a task, which, besides being life-threatening, almost certainly involved finding twelve dead sailors who had already been in the water for some time.

Tony had an idea of what Nico would be going through: 'Unfortunately, I have recovered a body before. So, I was able to tell the divers what it would be like and what they could expect.'

'It's different when you know you will definitely find a body. I didn't sleep the night before we were supposed to dive. It was quite stressful,' admitted Nico.

Nico had never seen a dead body in his life, never mind one that had been in the sea for two days and had possibly started to be consumed by crabs and other creatures. Not to mention having to transport a body — alone. He figured though, since he would be entirely alone inside the wreck, that he had no choice but to find a way to drag them that could be done solo. This would mean taking the dead sailors in his arms and carrying them out through the narrow passages of the wreck.

'I wouldn't say I was panicking, but I was definitely stressed about it. It was a very, very daunting prospect to get ready for.'

Next to Nico in the diving bell was Darryl Oosthuizen, who was diver 2. He was supposed to assist Nico in general, but his primary task would be to help handle the awkward umbilical (which supplied the diver's air and communication) that Nico was dragging into the wreck. Darryl would do this not inside the wreck, where Nico was, but just outside, where he would be safe from getting stuck. Even though this might seem the easier role, the job would undoubtedly be challenging, as the hose would be increasingly difficult to handle as Nico moved further into the wreck — going around corners, through doors, and up and down narrow stairs.

On regular saturation dives, it is the diver's own problem to handle their hose. These dives take place on the seabed, or an underwater structure like an oil rig, and the divers can easily manipulate their umbilicals themselves. Divers 1 and 2 work together solving their tasks, as there is no reason to help someone by handling their umbilical.

But this dive was very different. None of the team had ever dived into a wreck, or for that matter, any other enclosed structure. They had simply never done it — it isn't something sat divers are hired to do. It would be far too dangerous and complicated with the rigid umbilicals behind them and anyway is against the rules they follow. The rule is that sat divers must have visual contact with each other at all the times if they penetrate a structure. They certainly wouldn't be able to do that here, with Nico moving deep inside the wreck — going several floors up and down and through numerous closed doors — while Darryl remained outside. But as Tony explained it:

'We had to break some rules because that day everybody's heart ruled their head.'

On this dive, it was Darryl's task to control Nico's umbilical, easing it into the wreck when Nico moved inward, and pulling it out when Nico had to come back again or go somewhere else inside. In addition to assisting Nico when he could — for example by packing the bodies that Nico would hopefully find and pull out of the wreck so they could send them up safely to the diving ship — Darryl also had to be Nico's safety diver. It probably wouldn't make much difference since they would likely be separated in any crisis situation, with Nico inside the wreck and Darryl outside. But strictly speaking, he was still Nico's safety diver.

On this dive, André Erasmus would be the 'bellman.' This meant he had to stay inside the diving bell throughout and tend to the divers' needs. This would entail taking care of their gas supply, so the divers outside and inside the wreck had air to breathe. He would have to provide them with more or less cable, ensure the warm water in their suits was at the temperature they needed, and manage various other technical tasks from inside the bell.

André was the only one of the three who was not expecting to dive that day, but he had backup equipment with him that he could put on should he be forced to leave the bell. This would only happen in the most extreme of emergencies, as the man in the bell is crucial to the team — it is dangerous for everyone if he leaves his post.

They all knew their tasks. It was quiet in the bell as it approached the seabed thirty-four metres below the surface. They were lowered as close to the wreck as possible. Nico and Darryl opened the hatch at the bottom. It was so cramped that two of the divers had to crawl up the inside of the bell to make room for the hatch cover. One at a time, they dropped into the water under the bell. Here, there was a small platform where they could stand, still with their heads out of the water and inside the bell. Only at this point were their heavy and cumbersome diver's helmets secured. Once the helmets were mounted and it was confirmed that the radio, lights and breathing mixture of helium and oxygen were all working, the divers crawled into the open sea around them and released their long umbilicals. A platform had been lowered down next to them, containing tools and whatever else they might need. When both divers were ready, the next task was to find the wreck.

Even though their diving bell was positioned as close to the shipwreck as the underwater sonar system on the diving ship could get, there is often much poorer visibility on the seabed than, for example, seen in diving films on television. When Nico and Darryl emerged from the diving bell, the visibility was around ten metres, but there was no shipwreck in sight. This may sound strange if you haven't been on the seabed yourself. But even though the wreckage of *Jascon 4* was over thirty-one metres long and eleven metres wide, it is not that surprising that it might be impossible to see, even when very close. The divers had to use a compass to get there.

What follows is the original radio communication between Nico on the seabed and the control room on the diving ship.

Control Room: *Okay Nico, can you see the wreck?*
Nico: *Negative.*
Control Room: *Are you looking at your compass?*

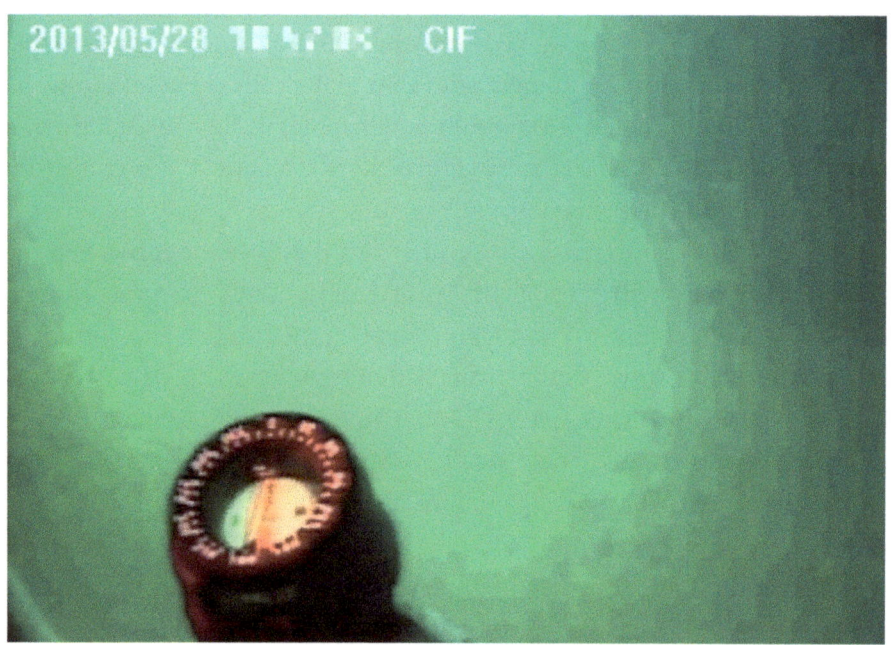

Authentic image from Nico's helmet camera.

Nico: *Yes... wait... I can see something. There it is.*
Control Room: *How far do you think it is?*
Nico: *Perhaps ten metres.*
Control Room: *You can climb on top of the diving bell and then jump to the wreck from there.*

Nico does as the control room suggests, climbs on top of the diving bell, and takes a leap towards the outline of the large wreck.

Control Room: *How far do you think it is from here?*
Nico: *Five metres.*

Only here—five metres from the wreck—can they see it lying on the seabed. On Nico's helmet camera, a section of the railing emerges from the murky water, and the ship's tyre fenders become clearer and clearer in the images Nico's helmet sends up to the diving control room.

Control Room: *Ah yes, I can see the wreck through your camera now. Okay. Which side is higher? The wreck is tilted, yeah?*

The divers climbed up onto the shipwreck and walked carefully along what had once been the ship's hull. And now they could begin the real task. But it wasn't as easy as it seemed. The relatively large ship had, as mentioned, ended up upside down. The wheelhouse and most of the front were buried in mud on the seabed and, because it had been sailing in the pirate-infested waters off Nigeria, all the doors were securely locked. The divers had no way of entering the ship.

The first task, therefore, was to find a suitable place to pry open a door, and dive control on the diving ship had already identified the best one for this purpose. But since the ship was upside down, they had to get Nico and Darryl all the way under the large wreck to find it.

Control Room: *Okay. Now I would like you to move down to the bottom of the wreck.*

The two divers let themselves fall from the top of the ship's hull and float down alongside it. They tried to orientate themselves on the way, simultaneously sending the best images up to dive control so that they could, with the help of the ship's blueprints, figure out their location on the wreck.

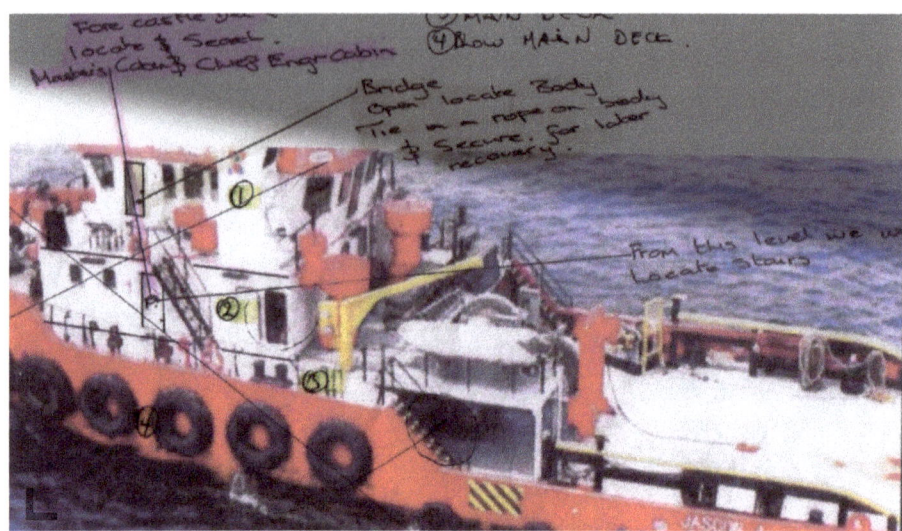

The diving manager's notes on a photo of the sunken ship.

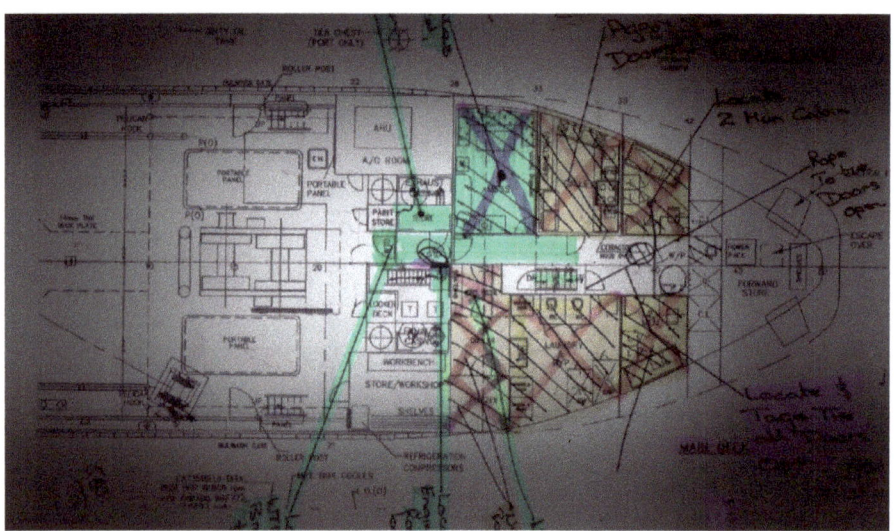

The diving manager's drawing of the search for bodies on the blueprint of the ship.

Control Room: *Just keep going... there's the railing, yeah?*

Nico has landed about halfway down the ship's side, where he holds onto the middle deck railing. There are windows, doors, lifeboats, stairs, winches and cranes — all upside down. He crawls down along the exterior of the wreck, while dive control watches through his helmet camera.

Control Room: *There's a window, isn't there... hmm? Okay, look to the left... and to the right. There should be some stairs if you go a bit further. Okay, you need to go a bit lower. What do we have there? Is that the stairs? Look for a door to your right... there should be a door.*

Nico has found the stairs. On the ship's blueprints there is a door under these stairs. The door should lead to the ship's mezzanine level from where, they have figured out, it will be possible to reach virtually all the rooms in the ship. Nico locates the door.

Control Room: *There's the door. Good. Alright... it is, of course, upside down. See if the door can be opened... Ah... locked. Okay... Okay, Darryl, are you there? Now I want you to go back to the bell and fetch all the tools. Okay, we need the crowbar, chisel and a hammer. Anything to open a door, okay?*

While Darryl heads back to the diver's working basket for the extra equipment that has been lowered down next to the diving bell, Nico takes stock of his surroundings.

Control Room: *Okay, and you're sure that's the right door, right?*
Nico: *Yep. Absolutely sure.*
Control Room: *Okay, excellent. Look, that's apparently the lock... there. Can you see the round, circular one? Let's get the wedge pounded into it and pry it open.*

In the meantime, Darryl returned from the diver's basket with a hammer, chisel and crowbar. They then tried to pound in the cylindrical lock, but the door on a ship is incredibly solid and it's extremely difficult to put proper force into a regular hammer underwater. Even though Nico worked hard for a long time, and Darryl tried to pry the door open with a large crowbar, it had only a minimal impact on the lock, which was designed to withstand pirate attacks. The relatively small hammer's pounding on the lock did beat off the handle and surround, but the door remained just as locked as before.

> **Control Room:** *What do you need? Do you want a bigger hammer?*
> **Nico:** *Yep. A bigger hammer would be really good.*
> **Control Room:** *A bigger hammer is on the way. We have a large sledgehammer up here on the deck. We're getting ready to lower it down to you.*

From the deck of the diving ship, a huge sledgehammer is lowered to the divers.

'I didn't stand a chance of breaking the door open with the regular hammer and chisel, as we had expected. But the hammer they sent down from the deck was the biggest hammer I'd ever seen. It looked like Thor's hammer, and even underwater, it was extremely heavy,' Nico recalls.

> **Control Room:** *Okay, just get into the wreck. Let's smash that door open.*

Although the new giant hammer leaves clear marks with each blow, the door remains unaffected and locked. Nico works hard and grows more and more tired, but the door doesn't budge.

> **Control Room:** *What kind of door did you say it was? Aluminium?*
> **Nico:** *No... I think it's steel.*
> **Control Room:** *Steel?... hmm... damn...*
> **Nico:** *Yeah.*
> **Control Room:** *Okay. Just keep going.*

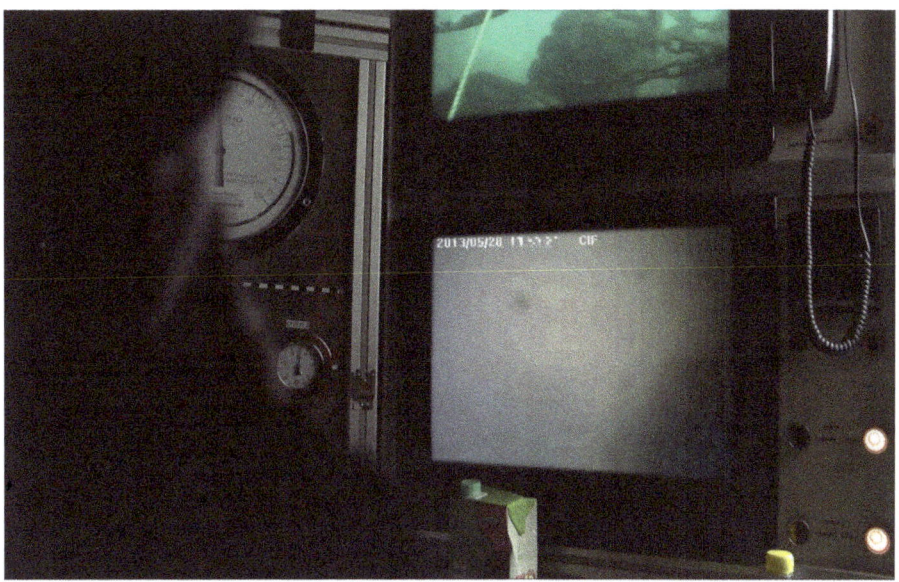

The view of the Diving Supervisor in the control room with screens showing images from divers' helmet cameras.

Diver Nico trying to pound open the locked door of the ship.

The divers had a tough task, as Tony explains: 'Ship doors are very often steel doors. They usually have multiple potential locking points plus an additional key lock. They need to withstand direct hits from large waves and endure enormous pressures. It's the strongest type of door you can get.'

> Nico and Darryl work for over an hour, and finally, they manage to bash the door so much that they can wedge a chisel into the lock and start breaking the door frame and lockbox.
>
> **Nico:** *Something's happening now...*
> **Control Room:** *Are you getting in? Is it open?*
> **Nico:** *Almost... it's getting there.*
>
> Nico gives the door some final hard blows with the large hammer, while Darryl leverages the lock with the crowbar. At last it works. The door gives way. It's hard to see what's happening on the divers' cameras, as hammering a huge door for an hour doesn't improve visibility, so dive control can't see what's going on.
>
> **Control Room:** *Is it open? And have you secured it, so it won't close on you?*
> **Nico:** *Negative.*
> **Control Room:** *Negative? What do you mean?*
> **Nico:** *It broke off.*
> **Control Room:** *Broke off? The whole door broke off?*
> **Nico:** *Yes.*
> **Control Room:** *Okay? So, no more door?*
> **Nico:** *That's right. No more door.*
> **Control Room:** *Okay... understood. Let me know when you're ready to go in.*

Nico and Darryl secured the large hammer and crowbar at the door's opening. Tools used underwater always have a string attached to the handle so they can be tied to your hand when in use and secured in place when finished with. Otherwise, they can easily disappear if dropped, and there was a good chance Nico would need the hammer and crowbar again if there were locked doors inside the wreck.

Tony was now thinking about next steps: 'When we got this far, we prepared to get a good overview of the wreck. We didn't know what we would be confronted with when Nico got in there. The only thing we had was the technical drawings of the vessel, which we had already gone through with the divers, so they would have an idea of what it would look like inside the ship.'

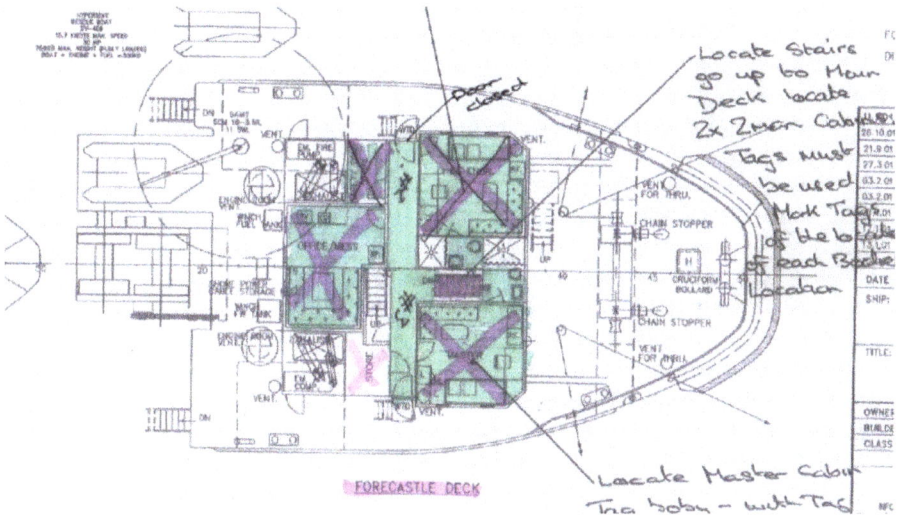

To avoid overlooking anything, all rooms were carefully marked, and the search plan was inscribed on the ship's drawings.

Tony had received floor plans of the tugboat and all its cabins so that the divers, and those in the control room guiding them, could orientate themselves through the wreck's many twists and turns.

'Our goal was to examine every cabin, living space, and generally any place where people could have been, so we could find all the deceased. Every time the diver investigated a compartment, we would mark it off on our drawings, so we wouldn't miss any of the bodies. They could be anywhere down there. But the fact that the wreck was upside down meant that we had to hold the drawings upside down and view them upside down to guide the divers correctly inside the wreck.'

They would flip the drawings and look at the back, which they held up to a lamp and illuminated, reversing them. Everything was upside down, right was left, left was right, etc. In the control room, through the camera mounted on his diving helmet, they could see what Nico could. They were trying to keep up with which way to lead him, so that nothing was overlooked.

Outside the wreck, Nico finished securing the tools. He checked his equipment and suit and gave the OK signal to Darryl, who gave an OK back. Nico looked into the dark hallway where they had broken off the door.

> It doesn't look particularly inviting. The corridor is narrow, no more than about ninety centimetres wide, and it is completely dark. Nico knows that many corners, doors, stairs, additional corridors and small cramped rooms await him, with his heavy equipment and the unwieldy but vital umbilical trailing behind him. He also knows that what he's about to start is not only life-threatening, it will also give him his first experience of seeing and touching a dead person. Something he definitely doesn't want to do and that will likely give him trauma for the rest of his life.
>
> **Control Room:** *Okay... Hmm... Nico? Are you ready to go in?*
> **Nico:** *Whatever...*
> **Control Room:** *All right... Good. Diver 1 is going in.*

Nico stepped forward with trepidation: 'So, when the door was open, I started searching for the sailors. I had no idea what I would encounter in there.'

Darryl grabbed Nico's thick umbilical and positioned himself outside the door, where he would stay for the rest of Nico's time inside the wreck. No one knew it at this point, but Darryl would stand there for the next eleven hours.

Nico was scared when he entered the dark corridor.

'I didn't look forward to it — going into a vessel that had just capsized... you don't know what you'll come across. You don't know if you'll get stuck in there... You're constantly in doubt about whether you made the right decision. It was really uncomfortable.'

Darryl took hold of Nico's umbilical, and slowly Nico started to walk into the inverted ship. Visibility inside the wreck was very poor. After a few steps,

Nico disappeared from Darryl's field of view.

Although visibility outside the wreck was about ten metres, things were entirely different on the inside. First of all, there was no natural light. Furthermore, everything had turned upside down when the ship capsized. Furniture, mattresses, fixtures, clothing, shoes and tools were strewn all about, some floating midwater, some with buoyancy that pressed them up against the top of the corridor.

Nico stumbled as he walked on what used to be the ceiling, but was now the floor. The visibility dropped to zero. Even though he had a torch on his helmet, its light was immediately absorbed by the murk in the already cloudy water in front of it. He had to feel his way and could see, at best, about half a metre in front of him. Nico grabbed hold of the inverted hand-rail in the narrow corridor and used it to navigate deeper into the dark shipwreck.

The risk was clear to Tony: 'A wreck lying upside down is a really, really dangerous place to be.'

When a ship has just sunk, it's not certain that it will stay where it is. A relatively complex ship of thirty-one metres length with several deck levels inside, like the one Nico was entering, would be very heavy and could settle on the seabed eventually. But often a heavy wreck slides down to a deeper spot on the seabed or suddenly leans to the side. Only when it has been on the bottom for a long time can anyone trust that it will stay where it is. *Jascon 4* had sunk only two days earlier, so no-one could be sure it wouldn't suddenly move while Nico was inside. There was no way to ensure that Nico wouldn't be injured if that happened. It didn't end there, as Tony explained:

'We knew that we had to get Nico into the wreck and there would be a significant risk associated with it. Outside, visibility wasn't so bad. But, of course, as soon as you entered the wreck, it was completely dark. The wreck was upside down. This was a recently sunken wreck. All the inventory, equipment, belongings and furniture that had been torn apart was floating around in a mess. Visibility was certainly not good. There are things one can get stuck in everywhere inside the darkness. It would be extremely dangerous — but there was no way around it.'

Navigating inside a wreck is not easy, even if it isn't upside-down. The corridors are narrow and everything in a ship is compressed to save space. The door frames are so tight that a person of Nico's size — even without diving gear — would have to sidle through them. Opening a door underwater — even if it's not locked — requires a lot of effort, as the water holds it and fallen debris can block it. There are an incredible number of rooms, corridors and stairs inside a ship like that. Even for someone familiar with its layout, it can be a labyrinth to navigate. Although Nico knew it would be dangerous, he was surprised at just how challenging it turned out.

'I only realized that when I looked into the wreck. If you look at the diving gear we had on, you will notice how much space someone like me takes up. It's really complicated. You have a kind of harness with all sorts of equipment on it, a huge helmet on your head with lights and cameras and wires, and you have a large backup dive tank on your back. You take up quite a bit of space when going through a narrow passage. Just turning around is almost impossible. You basically have to wiggle to get around … Because if you want to turn around inside the wreck, the corridors are so narrow that my backup dive tank on my back would almost be crushed against the wall on one side, while I was busy trying to manoeuvre on the other side.

'You are dragging this massive, thick air hose, the umbilical, along, and it won't bend much … so it's really hard to get around a corner, and there are plenty of those inside such a wreck. The cable is so stiff that it can't really bend ninety degrees. And all doors open inward. So, if you go through a door, and you don't keep the door open, the door will close again, thereby blocking your umbilical, and you get stuck. If that happens, you can't even go back to free it, because you would never be able to turn around and go back. So, I had small pieces of rope in my pocket. Every time I opened a door, I tied the handle to something to keep the door in the open position so that it wouldn't close on my umbilical.'

If the umbilical was damaged, it would mean not only that Nico wouldn't get air and light, but also that he would lose communication with the control room, which was his lifeline to the only people who knew the way out of the ship. He could never get out by 'feeling his way' in pitch darkness through a thirty-one-metre-long ship. But that wasn't the only thing that could go wrong, as Tony explained:

'The type of ship we were on, from which the diving bell hung, is controlled by satellite signals. There are no anchors at all. So, the large diving vessel only stays still as long as there is contact with the satellite.'

Nico knew it too: 'Everything is computer-controlled ... through satellite navigation, the ship's navigation system uses the ship's screws to keep the ship in the designated position. So, there's always a possibility of a "run-off." A run-off is when the vessel loses satellite connection and moves.'

Tony explained what would happen if the ship lost the satellite connection: 'We would have been in a very uncomfortable situation. The divers are attached to the diving ship itself via their air hoses. Their so-called umbilicals. If the ship moves on the surface, these umbilicals would drag the divers with it at the bottom of the sea.'

The impact this would have on the divers underwater, was clear to Nico: 'If the dive ship on the surface starts moving, your air hose won't stop the movement but will kill you by simply dragging you out through the vessel, following the dive ship. In the diving industry, you hear about vessels having a run-off, and divers being dragged along the seabed, and it's quite fine to be dragged along the seabed. There's nothing stopping you, and you just go along with the movement. But being dragged through the innermost part of a shipwreck, through door openings, and up and down metal stairs... I would have broken every single bone in my body.'

Surely this was all unlikely to actually occur? Tony was circumspect: 'It can happen, and it has happened. It would be extremely dangerous. I mean, there's no doubt about it. It would be... Yeah... I don't even want to think about it, to be honest.'

Inside the wreck, Nico didn't have that luxury: 'That's one of the reasons why we usually never enter wrecks. Every time there was a little creak or another sound of metal moving somewhere, which happens all the time in a recently sunken wreck... you know, a "dink" or "donk," I would stop and take a break, and I was basically just waiting for something terrible to happen. Every time I heard something, I thought, "Now it's happening!" So, it was a bit... a bit stressful. It was in the back of my mind all the time.'

It was a calculated gamble for Tony: 'It's a real risk. I mean, you're entirely dependent on everyone working with you when you're the one who has to be alone inside such a wreck... We knew what we were doing was dangerous, but we tried to make it as safe as possible for the divers, and everyone agreed that it was important to retrieve these dead sailors, so they could be buried by their loved ones. So, we agreed that we had to bend the rules a bit.'

Naturally, Nico did not know the layout of the tugboat. He had seen drawings of the interior, but even if he had been able to memorize the plans, it would have mattered little since he couldn't see anything inside the wreck. He was entirely dependent on the team on the dive ship to navigate for him.

'It's hard to understand it if you're not in it… that everything… except yourself, is basically upside down in this wreck. So, everything was reversed. If you go left in a passage, you are actually going right on the ship's interior floor plan. If you open a door, the door handle naturally opens downward, but all doors on the vessel open upward because it's upside-down. But when you grab the handle, you always try it the wrong way first. All ordinary things one is used to… just had to be turned 180 degrees in the head… It was very disorienting…'

The umbilical that Nico dragged behind him inside the *Jascon 4* was very long. It ran all the way to him from the diving bell, which was hanging in the water column somewhere outside the wreck. But, as previously described, they are so stiff and unmanageable that it is a challenge to turn. Going around a sharp corner with the cable hanging after you is practically impossible.

Nico realized that, when he had to go back through the narrow passages, he would often have to do it backwards, while Darryl, outside, pulled the cable. It meant that Nico and Darryl had to have radio contact all the time, so Darryl knew when to feed more cable to Nico as he went further into the wreck, and when to pull the cable outward, as Nico went the other way.

Nico and Darryl were mostly very far from each other. The cable often went around many corners, through cabins and up and down stairs. Sometimes it led to entirely different floors from where Darryl was standing outside the wreck. Darryl couldn't go into the wreck himself, but had to stay just outside the door and help with Nico's cable. Otherwise, it would have quickly gotten stuck somewhere deep inside the wreck. It would be a long and extremely dangerous dive for Nico.

> **Control Room:** *Okay, Nico, let's go down this corridor. Look for cabin doors on both sides, okay?*
> **Nico:** *Here's a door… I'm going in…*

Control Room: *Roger. Look around... if there are any bodies in there. They will probably float above you at this stage... Keep checking up under the ceiling, over.*
Nico: *Roger... Going further in...*
Control Room: *Okay, um... We are expecting to find a body here.*

Sat divers have the significant advantage over scuba divers that they can theoretically stay submerged as long as they want, since they receive their air supply through a hose from their ship. However that advantage is also a drawback. The umbilical is exactly what it sounds like. What comes through that cable is absolutely vital for the diver, much like the umbilical cord is for a foetus. If it gets caught, stuck, or damaged inside a shipwreck, the diver dies. Nico knew this.

'The umbilical... if I say it's your lifeline, that's an understatement. If my umbilical got cut in this wreck, I wouldn't make it out of the water alive. Everything you need to survive is inside that. You have your warm water to heat up the suit, your radio communication, your air, your light. The light is very important... and the light from my helmet was the only light source in the wreck. So, if my cable was cut, there would be no light either. Everything would be pitch-black... you can't do anything. I would never find my way out in the darkness.'

Interestingly, sat divers do not utilise the same backup equipment as regular divers. A scuba diver would never dive without a backup regulator for their breathing gas supply, which can also be used to assist other divers if they run short of air. They'd also never sensibly dive into a wreck (or any other confined space) without a backup torch. But sat divers don't do that. If their light breaks, they go back to the diving bell and have it repaired. They do carry backup air tanks on their backs, but they only last about ten minutes and it would take much longer than that to get out of this wreck. Even if Nico managed to escape the wreck using his emergency cylinder, Darryl wouldn't have been able to provide him with any more to breathe once he got out. Sat divers simply don't carry air for sharing. As he explains, Nico also wouldn't be able to swim to the surface while breathing from his backup tank.

'If I swam to the surface, I would die before reaching it because of the gas buildup inside me. You know, decompression sickness... I would probably die instantly. And if I had to use my emergency air inside the wreck... if the cable got damaged, I wouldn't make it out alive.'

Nico looks directly at me. 'That's it.'

In other words, sat divers are simply not designed for the kind of operations Nico was now deeply involved in, as Tony explained:

'Penetrating a wreck with a thick umbilical behind you is a risk. It's about controlling the umbilical so it doesn't get twisted or caught in anything. It's quite difficult. And if you penetrate a wreck, it has to be handled very carefully. It's quite dangerous, and if something happens while he's in there... well... it's not good.'

Nico compared it with popular images of diving: 'If you watch *Discovery Channel* and those kinds of places, you see those fancy divers swimming through wrecks and whatnot. It's not the same. This is one hundred per cent different. This wreck was a terrible place to be. It was like walking into a nightmare. Everywhere you went, if you went through a small passage, you were kicking up mud, you couldn't see anything in there. There were things that could fall on top of you. It was just a terrible experience. Honestly, you shouldn't be penetrating anything. Look at me... I'm not a small guy. It's not easy for me to fumble around inside an upturned wreck with zero visibility in complete darkness...'

It may sound strange that it would be so difficult to enter the wreck, especially since there were two divers involved simultaneously, and Darryl was supposed to be Nico's safety diver outside the wreck. Wasn't there a safety plan? Couldn't Darryl help?

Nico shakes his head.

'If something went wrong, the plan was for Darryl to enter the wreck to assist me. But now, looking back and having gained much more experience than I had back then... I can see that it wouldn't have been a real possibility. Not at all. The problem is, that if you send the diver from the outside into the wreck, then there are two divers inside, and no-one is tending to their umbilicals. If Darryl went in to help me, his umbilical would get stuck somewhere immediately, as he wouldn't have anyone outside to manage it, and he probably would never have even reached me. It would have been fatal for both of us. So, the idea that Darryl could have rescued me simply wasn't a possibility.'

Tony could see that: 'We knew it was tricky... but we still had a standby diver in the dive bell, who had a spare suit and a helmet, so he could assist, if there was a serious emergency for the two divers.'

Nico wasn't convinced: 'It was a good plan — in theory, but it would never work in reality. André, the standby diver inside the dive bell... he would then have had to put on his gear, put on the spare helmet and jump out of the bell. He would have had to tend to both mine and Darryl's umbilicals from outside the wreck — plus his own... it would never work. Tending one umbilical is difficult. Tending three is impossible. We would just have had three divers stuck in different places. The ship could not have sent more divers to help us, because the three of us were connected to the diving bell. So the ship would not have been able to hoist up the bell after more divers. No. That would not work. No one would have been able to come and help me inside. Realistically... if I couldn't get out myself from inside, I would probably have died.'

Nico had to be extremely careful and hope that the air hose wouldn't get stuck inside the wreck. But sometimes, that's just not enough...

Control Room: *Okay, are you in there, Nico?*
Nico: *I'm outside the door.*
Control Room: *Which door is that?*
Nico: *It's a cabin... there's a porthole on the right.*
Control Room: *A porthole...? There shouldn't be any portholes there...*
Nico: *Well, there is...*
Control Room: *Full stop. You do know where you are, right?*
Nico: *Yes... I'm on the bridge... I think.*
Control Room: *On the bridge? Are you sure? Can you see? Do you have any visibility at all, can you see anything, Nico?*
Nico: *No...*
Control Room: *Can you show me the door you just opened?*
Nico: *That's the door I opened.*
Control Room: *Okay, there's a name on it. Show me the nameplate... Aha... it says 'Chief Engineer.' It's the chief engineer's door.*
Nico: *Roger.*

> **Control Room:** *Okay, let's open that, please. I can see on the drawing that... when you enter the door, it gets very tight. It's a really small cabin. I can imagine that everything in the cabin has fallen into the small corner and is scattered all over the place.*
> **Nico:** *Roger... I'm going in.*

Dive control was right. The reason Nico couldn't open the door was because something had moved and was blocking the doorway. When, with difficulty, he finally pushed the door open and squeezed inside he discovered why it had been so hard.

'I had to push the door open. And when I went in, something very heavy fell and blocked the door... it landed on my air hose, so it got stuck. So... because of that... I was helplessly stuck inside. And it was certainly not a nice, spacious cabin... I was stuck and couldn't move. I couldn't turn around and I couldn't go backwards. And I couldn't get out because something was now blocking the door behind me.'

The sediment inside the cabin had been stirred up and Nico had zero visibility. It might as well have been pitch dark. He couldn't turn around and remove what had fallen on his umbilical, its stiffness prevented it.

He tried to keep panic out of his voice when he reported to the dive vessel up on the surface.

> **Nico:** *I have a problem...*
> **Control Room:** *A problem?*
> **Nico:** *I'm stuck in here.*
> **Control Room:** *Excuse me? What?*
> **Nico:** *I'm stuck. Something fell on my umbilical.*
> **Control Room:** *Stuck?*
> **Nico:** *Yes, and it has pinned my umbilical against the door. The door is closed.*
> **Control Room:** *Okay... can you move what's on your umbilical?*
> **Nico:** *Negative. Can't turn around.*
> **Control Room:** *Okay, this is not good.*
> **Nico:** *No.*

Then you hear Nico trying to move around. But he can't help himself.

Control Room: *Okay, Nico? I'm with you.*

From here, there is no more talk for a while. Nico tries to free himself, and groans. He's working hard. There are bumps and something creaking. His breathing deepens and becomes faster and faster.

Dive control follows along on Nico's camera. Furniture and sediment are stirred up, making it almost impossible to see anything other than Nico's hands and occasionally a corner of some kind of white furniture.

'It was a very small room I was in,' Nico recounted. 'When I realized I was stuck in there, I panicked.'

There's one thing that all divers fear — and usually they are really good at avoiding it — and that is panic. Panic is one of the most dangerous things one can experience because the body reacts irrationally and often illogically. A lot of energy is spent on the wrong things and one often makes the wrong decision instead of relaxing and thinking things through.

Nico's situation was extremely uncomfortable — he was effectively trapped deep inside the wreck — unable to turn around and fix the problem, knowing that no-one could help him get out. In such situations, one is entirely dependent on those around for assistance. Unfortunately, in Nico's case, they were far away, with no way of helping him out, and they could only provide advice. Which is precisely what they did. The diving supervisors on the ship were at least as shaken as Nico, but they didn't let on. The voice in Nico's radio from the ship remained calm and, although there wasn't much they could do to help, that calmness in Nico's ear helped him to relax and think.

'I tried to control my level of panic. But it wasn't easy.'

Control Room: *Okay, how are you, Nico? Just talk to me, and I'll help you. You have to push against the cabin. Just keep pushing. We are here with you.*

The only way out was to go backwards, but something lay on top of his umbilical and Nico had no idea what it was. It made it impossible for him to turn around. Moreover, whatever it was was very heavy and it had blocked the door and closed it. Dive control didn't have many solid pieces of advice. Nico's breathing and the bumps on the audio from the radio communication show that he was struggling hard with something.

'What I tried, besides thrashing around in panic... was to try to remove the things blocking, so I could turn around a bit. I finally managed to turn enough to see that it was a large freezer that had fallen on my umbilical and at the same time it had closed the door. It was now blocking the door, pinching my umbilical, and making it impossible for me to get out... or move. However, I was able to get one hand under the freezer and lift it enough to turn around and grab it with both hands. And then I could lift the freezer, so my umbilical was free, and I could move a bit again.'

The way Nico handled the situation is truly impressive. Especially since this was only his second dive in that kind of sat equipment. It was very different from the diving gear he had previously trained to use.

> **Control Room:** *Are you winning?*
> **Nico:** *Yes... I think I can get out now...*

Most people would have probably reacted differently and, even though Nico went into a bit of a panic, he did the right thing and managed to get out unharmed. Although 'out' might be a bit of an overstatement. He was still deep inside the tight, dark wreck, and his task had only just begun.

'I managed to open the door. It was the biggest relief I've ever had in my life. I panicked a bit, I must say. When the freezer tipped and squeezed my umbilical, I seriously considered whether it was the right thing to dive around inside this wreck. Because honestly, I thought, "This is it... This will be the last time anyone sees me."'

'It was unusual circumstances,' Tony concluded. 'Being so isolated and being so deep and so far inside an upturned wreck is really, really dangerous. It's not the kind of thing you normally plan to do. We bent the rules way too much, because we believed it was the right thing to do, and no decisions were rational.'

Nico found it emotionally wearing. 'I really didn't like being in there.

It was definitely something we had to do ... get the dead guys out ... But throughout the dive, I just thought about everything that could go wrong. It was really stressful.'

If it had been a dive on a normal job, they would probably have given Nico a break and made sure he was okay before continuing. But this was not an ordinary dive and Nico continued without a break, moving deeper into the wreck.

'I had no children at that time. But now that I have children, I would undoubtedly make a different decision.'

5

Treading on a Mattress or a Body Feels Just the Same

Nico moved deeper and deeper into the wreck. He often had to grope his way, since there was frequently no visibility at all and he risked stumbling over furniture or fixtures that had come loose.

'Obviously, I'm in there to find a corpse. To search for the dead bodies.'

Nico knew that what he had agreed to was something he had hoped never to experience. But now it wasn't a question of whether it would happen or not... he knew that very soon he would see dead bodies, and he would have to touch them. Not just once, but many times. There were twelve drowned sailors inside the wreck. Twelve bodies that he had to retrieve.

Nico had entered a medium-sized room where some furniture had been tossed around, making it difficult to tell one thing from another. He had to feel his way through everything that lay on the floor, which was originally the ceiling. It was challenging to navigate through all the clutter. Nothing could be ignored, so he crawled slowly, searching the room for bodies. Some things he picked up, others he touched and felt. In the control room, they followed along on his helmet camera.

> **Control Room:** *Look up. They might be above you... they've been there so long that some of them may have updrift by now... is there anything above you?*
> **Nico:** *No. Only some kind of cabinet... or shelf.*
> **Control Room:** *What is this to your left? Is it a body?*
> **Nico:** *It's a chair.*
> **Control Room:** *A chair, okay... What's down there? At your feet.*

Nico almost has to lie down in the cluttered room to investigate.

Nico: *It's a mattress.*
Control Room: *Their mattress, yes. You're in the four-man cabin.*
Control Room: *Hmm, I think you better prepare yourself to find a body in there, okay?*

Nico was now in one of the areas on the ship where they knew there must have been one or more crew members present when the ship went down. It was only a matter of time before he found the first body. But how does one get ready to handle a corpse?

'I tried to prepare myself mentally. But ... there was really nothing I could do ... You know it will happen if you go into such a wreck ... that's why I was there. I would rather not have done it, but it was something that had to be done.'

Nico continued his search and reached the bridge. Just like everywhere else in the wreck it was pitch-black, but there wasn't as much clutter, since most of this room's fixtures were bolted to the floor — which was now the ceiling. But not everything was up above him.

'If you step on a mattress ... I can tell you now, that stepping on a mattress and stepping on a dead body's thigh — it feels exactly the same. So, there were many times when I stepped on something and it sent shivers down my spine, and I stuck my hand down, and I felt: "Ah ... It's just a mattress." It happened several times ... And a couple of times ... it wasn't a mattress ...'

Nico sits still for a moment, staring into nothingness. A moment passes before I realize what he means.

'The first one I found was on the bridge ...'

The area Nico was in had been at the top of the ship. Now, naturally, it was at the bottom and had sunk quite a bit into the mud on the seabed. So mud had already begun to seep into the wreck, and a fine layer of silt lay everywhere. As Nico moved forward, it immediately started swirling.

'I moved quite slowly, and you could see that the mud had already started to come in everywhere. And as I walked down the hallway ... that's why I know that stepping on a corpse is like stepping on a mattress ... it feels the same. And suddenly, I could feel it: There was a body.'

Nico leaned forward and grabbed a shoulder. As he gently pulled it towards him, he uncovered the body of a strongly built man in a checked shirt, lying along one wall, partially buried in the mud. As Nico touched the man, the mud swirled away — and Nico found himself staring directly into the face of the dead man, presumably the ship's captain. He'd had a nosebleed, but otherwise looked completely peaceful. Peaceful… but dead. Nico was in shock but professional enough not to show it. That was why he was there, and he continued, seemingly unaffected, working on some kind of autopilot.

Nico: *I've found one.*
Control Room: *Okay, you found one, yeah?*
Nico: *Roger.*
Control Room: *Okay, we're taking the body out, yeah?*
Nico: *I'm taking the body out.*
Control Room: *Okay. Yes.*

There was no way around it. Nico was entirely alone inside the wreck, so he had to get the body out single-handedly. He took hold under the dead man's arms and lifted him, to pull him all the way out through the wreck. Even though the body had only been in the wreck for a few days, a certain stiffness had set in, and the man's strong arms were in an 'embrace position' in front of him. A large enough man as it was, this made his body especially difficult to manoeuvre through the cramped passages.

Many of the early times I spoke to Nico, he told me quite coolly of the experience of finding, dragging and packing up the bodies. But as we became closer and went over the story multiple times, I realized that he talked about it 'routinely' — he always used the same phrases and expressions when referring to what had obviously been very challenging down in the wreck. He talked about it quite lightly as 'just something that had to be done.' He had told the story so often that he could tell it in a way that he was used to, and therefore it did not upset him anymore.

Nico had trained to weld and build underwater. He wasn't trained for what it would be like to see a dead body and by no means trained to handle one. So, as we got to know each other, I started asking him questions in different ways, so he couldn't answer in the way he was used to, but had to think and remember how he had felt in different situations. He suddenly became intensely affected when talking about the bodies. Even then, his responses were quite matter-of-fact, but you could see how deeply he was impacted and probably still traumatized by the experience.

'You think you're mentally strong… until you're asked to do something like that, and even when you agree to do it, you think, "Oh, I can handle this, I should be able to." And when you touch the body, when you find someone, there's nothing that can prepare you for the initial shock and emotional overwhelm of actually seeing someone who is dead and having to handle the body… And it was just, ugh, it was a horrible experience.'

Nico eventually got the body all the way out and Darryl, the safety diver waiting there, grabbed the legs so they could lift it into a 'diving cage' lowered from the ship. The cage is usually used to hoist divers and equipment up and down, but now it was equipped with body bags and ropes. Once securely loaded with its grim cargo, the cage could be hoisted up to the ship.

> **Control Room:** *Okay, do we have a body bag?*
> **Nico:** *Yes, I have a bag.*

I asked Nico what goes on inside your head in such a situation and how he managed to go through with it.

'It's hard to explain, but you have to … of course, it's a human being, but you have to get it out of your mind, and you have to try to focus on just putting "something" inside a bag.'

Tony explained the process: 'We were provided with body bags on the way there. And each of the bodies we found was put into a body bag by the two divers and then hoisted up to the surface, where we had a refrigerated container.'

Nico: 'It is… It really hurt… emotionally.'

> Darryl and Nico had now got the dead man into the cage, and they took out a body bag and unfolded it.
>
> **Control Room:** *Okay, so we're putting him in a bag, and it will be body bag No. 1, Roger?*
> **Nico:** *Roger, understood.*

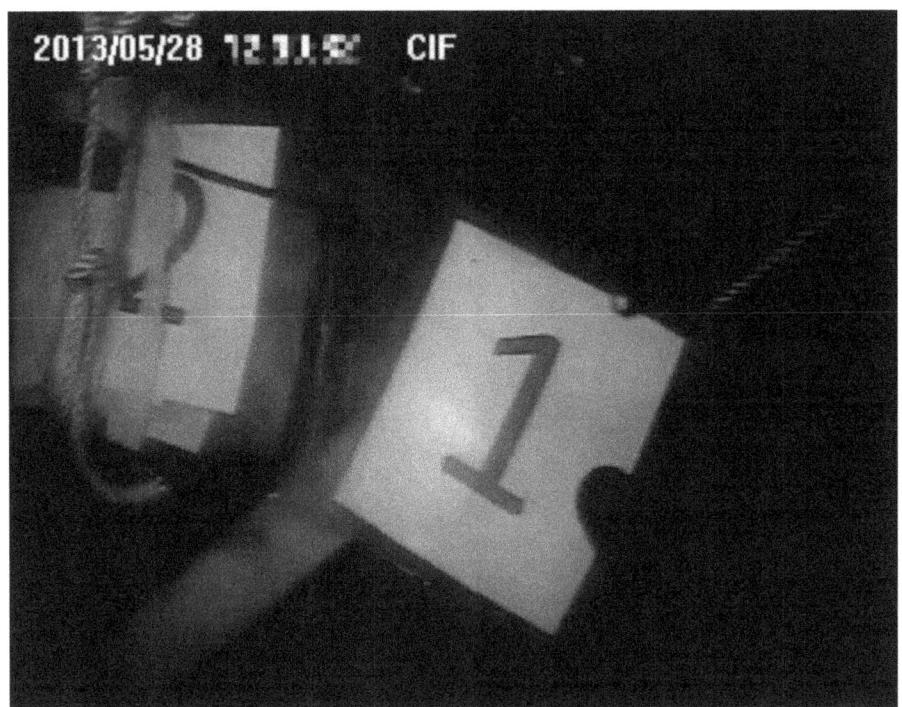

Image from Nico's helmet camera of the numbers they put on the body bags.

Nico found a bundle of laminated sheets of paper with numbers hanging inside the cage. He took out sheet No. 1 and attached it to the body bag with zip ties.

Nico and Darryl had trouble handling the dead man. It was surprisingly difficult to get him into the black body bag.

'Rigor mortis had apparently already set in, so it was difficult to move… to manipulate the body. Darryl and I really had to use force to fold the arms in and had to use ropes to keep the arms close to the body, so we could get the body into the bag.

'I think there are people built for that kind of thing… I'm not one of them. The experience will stay with me for the rest of my life. I mean… of course, it was something we had to do, but it was… I wouldn't… hmm… I wouldn't wish that on my worst enemy. It was terrible.'

After explaining the last part, Nico sits silently for a moment and you can see that his mind is back in the diver's cage, as they pack one body after another into bags. He looks a troubled man, with his big teddy bear-like body and his normally very sympathetic, smiling face. I feel sorry for him. He really is a kind and helpful man and I feel bad that he has to relive all this just because I want to hear his story. I let him sit for a while and recover before we continue.

> **Control Room:** *Okay, when we're done, we go back to the wreck, and we keep looking for more dead bodies on the bridge, right? Nico? Are you going in again?*
> **Nico:** *Yep. I'm ready.*

Although everyone knew that the experience was terrible for Nico and Darryl, it was what they had come for. As soon as they were done packing up the first body, securing and fastening it to the diver's cage, Nico went back into the wreck to find the remaining eleven sailors.

> **Control Room:** *Okay, let's go down that passageway there. And let's head towards the captain's cabin. The door will be on the left side. Remember, you're going slightly downhill now, right?*
> **Nico:** *Yes, Roger.*
> **Control Room:** *It feels like you're sliding down the passageway, doesn't it?*
> **Nico:** *Yes, that's right.*

Nico moved slowly down a long passageway. With the ship slightly tilted and the stern much lower in the mud than the bow, so the wheelhouse protruded at the front of the ship.

> **Control Room:** *Okay... is it the right place?*

On the side of the passageway there is a chrome railing.

> **Control Room:** *Okay, there's the railing. Just put your hand on the railing and follow it... keep going.*

As Nico grabs the railing, his foot hits something.

Nico: [Says something unintelligible].
Control Room: *What are you saying?... Are you at the bottom?*
Nico: *No... I found a body.*
Control Room: *You found a body. Okay. In the passageway, right?*
Nico: *In the passageway. Yes.*

Nico bends down and grabs the collar of a young man in a blue boiler suit. As he pulls him, the man sits up. The body's movements look strange and lively, but it's clear from the look in the man's face, that he is dead. He also has a nosebleed and blood from his ears. He looks strangely peaceful.

Nico lifts him up and starts walking backwards. Painstakingly, Nico drags the dead man in a firm embrace all the way out through the narrow passageways of the ship. As he approaches the exit, Darryl steps in and helps get the body into the cage.

Control Room: *Okay, okay. One of you grab the collar, one grabs the feet. Okay? Make sure his clothes don't come off when we pull him up.*

Darryl and Nico struggle to get the dead man out of the ship and down from the railing toward the diver's cage. It sounds simple when you describe what they are doing, but you have to remember that this is happening at the bottom of the Atlantic Ocean. If they lose their grip on the dead man they will never see him again. Right where the divers' helmet lights shine, it's bright and it's easy to navigate in the surroundings. But just ten metres away there is complete darkness, and they wouldn't have a chance in hell of finding anything in the vast ocean surrounding them. They wouldn't have a clue where to look.

Control Room: *Okay, when you get him in the cage, make sure you have his body tied and secure. So, he doesn't float away from you, copy?*
Nico: *Roger that.*

As we talk, something dawns on Nico. Something that hadn't occurred to him before.

'It surprises me that everyone else was just like… "Let's just get on with this." And from the ship, it was just: "Okay, let's get him out of there and get him in the bag and blah, blah, blah. Make sure the body doesn't float away… like this and that." As if it was just a completely ordinary job that needed to be done… but it wasn't.'

In the pictures from the helmet cameras, you see Darryl and Nico manipulating the body as if it were a tool they are working with. They do exactly what they are told over the radio.

> **Control Room:** *We're putting ropes down along the sides of the cage, so you can tie him to the cage, right?*
>
> Nico and Darryl get the dead man into the cage and start unrolling a new body bag.

Nico pauses in his narrative.

'Seeing that person in the water, looking at that person's face, you know that… it's a human. That person has a family. Just thinking about it… it's tough.'

> Nico unzips the black body bag, and they start struggling with the body. It is difficult to handle because it's so unwieldy, but they patiently manage to fit it into the bag.

Even Tony, who is generally one of the calmest people I've ever talked to, is visibly affected when discussing this part of their task. And he was up in the ship's dive control while it was happening. But when I ask how he felt about it, surprisingly, considering how cool he usually is, he gets teary-eyed.

'It was the same for everyone. Everyone gave everything they had to find as many of these drowned sailors as we possibly could. If they'd just disappeared somewhere in the deep, and no-one ever sees them again… It's even more traumatic for the loved ones than if they'd drowned. It was important to get them up. But it was also tough for us up on the ship. The bodies came up one at a time and had to be handled up there. And there you don't have the water to take away most of the smell. There you have the actual weight of the body, and you are reminded that they ... these are real people with families and children who will never see them again.'

Nico and Darryl have already become less fumbling in their movements, and getting the body into the bag is faster this time. They talk less and work in silence.

Nico recounts, 'It was strange ... it's like ... "We need to get that person in a bag, get him up, put him in a container, done. Go into the wreck and look for the next one." But the enormous shock, the stress that I experienced while doing it, was ... it was horrible. It was much more than I had imagined it would be.'

Even though you can't see Nico and Darryl's faces inside their large diving helmets, you can tell from their body language that something is wrong. They work efficiently, but they are both in a state of shock. They say as little as possible and their movements are zombie-like.

Control Room: *How are you guys feeling? Are you okay?*
Nico and Darryl: *Yes. Yes, yes.*
Control Room: *It's not affecting you too much?*

The divers continue working in silence.

Control Room: *Have any of you done this kind of thing before?*
Nico: *Negative.*
Control Room: *This is the first time?*
Nico: *Yes.*
Control Room: *Okay, is he in the bag? Mark him.*
Nico: *He's ready ... we're done.*
Control Room: *Done?*
Nico: *Yes.*
Control Room: *Okay, let's get you back on the wreck, and we'll bring the cage with the body up. Okay?*

Nico: *Roger.*

Nico crawls back into the wreck, and now things start to move quickly. He enters the passageway where the crew attempted to escape through the locked door, and there he finds a sailor who couldn't get out.

'The first one was, of course, the worst because it's something you've never done before. The second one is a bit easier. And by the third, it was just: out with them — up in the cage, into the bag, number on the body bag... up on the dive vessel. But that was only because we kept ourselves busy and tried to see it as something completely different than what it was.' Nico recalls.

Nico lifts the dead sailor and pulls him out through the wreck. The sailor has no shoes on, and Nico holds him by his bare feet, which are the first things Darryl encounters outside the wreck.

Nico: *One more... at the door in the passageway.*
Control Room: *Okay, Nico... you take him out feet first, right?*
Nico: *Roger.*
Control Room: *Okay, understood.*

Routinely Nico and Darryl lift the shoeless man into the cage and open a body bag.

Control Room: *Okay, we found body No. 3, by the watertight door in the passageway.*

The divers place the dead man in the bag and label it.

Tony's summary of what they found hints at an unusual sinking: 'Out of the total of twelve crew members aboard when the ship sank, we found eleven bodies. They were in corridors, by doors, some in cabins... It looked like everyone tried to get out, but the doors were locked and it apparently sank so fast that nobody had a chance to get out. It's very rare that something like this happens. Usually, some people escape... at least those standing up in the wheelhouse. They had open doors because of the heat and could close them if pirates were coming, but still, they didn't get out. It must have sunk violently and incredibly fast.'

6

Grace, Grace, Grace

Less than thirty metres from where Nico picked up the last dead sailor, but on a different deck inside the wreck, sat Harrison. However, he might as well have been on the moon, because nobody knew he was there and he had no idea that divers were on the wreck. It could have taken several days for the divers to think to search where he was and, even if they did, Harrison was as far inside the wreck as you could get. Not exactly the first place a diver might visit. Or perhaps ever would.

> Harrison has other things on his mind since there's little oxygen left in his compartment. He struggles with every breath, sucking up what little remains in the thick atmosphere.

'After a while, it started to become very difficult to breathe. It's like... at first, I could breathe normally... then it became a bit harder, and eventually, I really struggled with each breath... and I noticed that the water inside the cabin was rising... it slowly rose in there. There was less air... and more water,' Harrison recalls.

> Harrison feels that his small air pocket is disappearing. He's used up nearly all the oxygen in there, and he is not just imagining the rising waters.
> It seems the wreck has either moved a bit since it sank, or there is a leak somewhere, allowing water to push the air out. In any case, the water level is steadily rising in Harrison's tiny enclosure. The water, which used to reach some of the way up the door frame, is now all the way up to the top of the door against Harrison's ceiling—once the floor—of the second engineer's cabin.

Harrison remembers how it felt, 'When I started having trouble breathing, I realized that the air inside was running out. I had to force myself to breathe, like stretching your lungs to their limit to suck in the air. I expected it to be over very soon because I started feeling dizzy, like I wanted to sleep. But if I passed out, I would be the first job of a crayfish. When someone dies in the water, crabs and crayfish usually eat the eyes, tongue, ears, nose. It happens very quickly. And I thought that if I die, I don't think there's anyone who can take care of my wife better than I can. I just thought, "Oh, she's going to suffer." This just ran through my head, and I thought about how my mother and my wife would feel. I thought about those two.'

The other sailors in the ship were not visibly attacked by any animals, so this might be a horror scenario of Harrison's own making. Maybe that's a thought you get when you're sitting alone in the dark, 102 feet below the surface, with almost no oxygen. While it is true that crabs, crayfish and other marine scavengers play a crucial role in the marine ecosystem by breaking down organic matter, including dead bodies, and that soft tissues are eaten first, that was not something that happened on board *Jascon 4*.

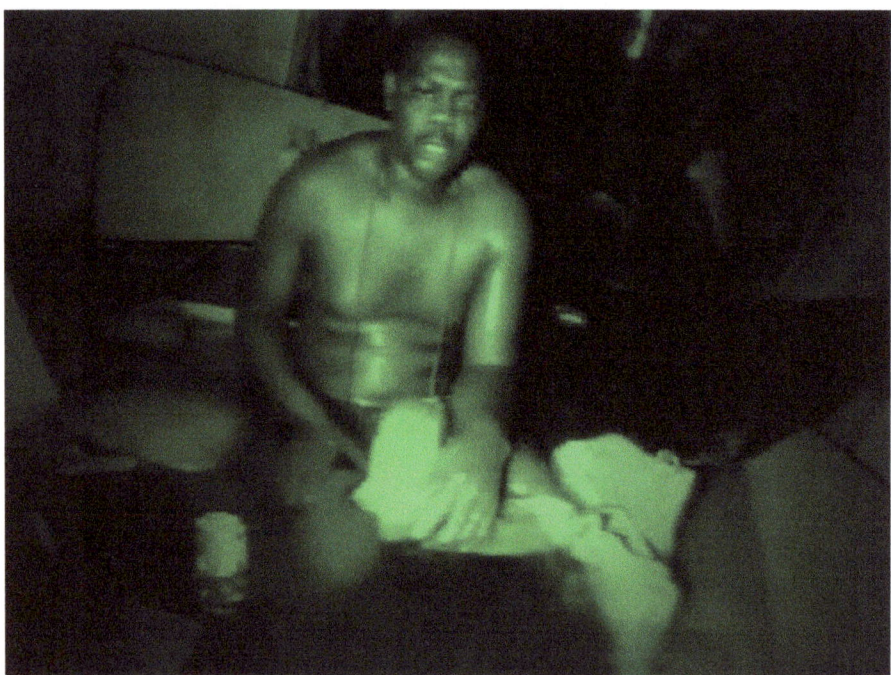

Authentic picture of Harrison in the air pocket.

Harrison's movements are sluggish. Even though he tries, he can't move very fast. His breathing is wheezy, and every gulp of air is a struggle. Because the water has risen, it's impossible for him to keep much of his body out of the water. The 'crabs' attack his body underwater, but he can't muster the strength to fight back. Yet, he finds a means to endure in the darkness.

'When I sing... it's like I get the panic off me. So... I sang.'

One of the last times I interviewed Harrison, he suddenly brought up the singing. He hadn't talked about it on the other occasions that we discussed his time in the cabin. I asked him what he sang. He stared blankly into the air and sat like that for a while. Then suddenly, he started singing.

'Invisible God.
Thou are the miracle worker.
You are worthy,
oh Lord.
You are worthy,
oh Lord.'

Harrison sang beautifully. It was a kind of gospel song, and his voice suggested he had sung that song many times. But there was also an incredibly melancholy tone to the way he sang it. His eyes were completely lifeless. Normally during the interviews, he was a lively storyteller with enthusiasm and humour in his eyes, despite the story he was telling. When he sang for me in that small interview studio, in a strange house in Lagos, Nigeria, with an ugly green screen background and four lights shining directly into his face, it was incredibly moving. Mentally, he was back in the cabin of the overturned ship.

We sat in silence for a while. He didn't look at me. He gazed into the distance. Then he started to cry. Tears ran down his cheeks as he slowly began to sing another song.

Harrison in our interview studio in Lagos, Nigeria.

'Grace, grace, grace.
I see grace.
Grace, grace, grace.
All I see is grace.
Grace, grace, grace…'

He stopped and cried a little. Then he looked at me, seemingly trying to explain what was happening.

'I'm just … back in the cabin … [crying] … in that situation again … the days I had been there … because I know with my strength … with my strength alone, I would never get out … alone, I can't do it … not alive.'

He sat for a while with that vacant look in his eyes again.

'One thought kept running through my head: That I had to stay alive. Alive, to see my children again … see tomorrow … and to see my future … my children. See my children again.'

It is difficult to describe that situation, where Harrison began to sing and tried to let me in on what was going on inside him in the upturned cabin … but it was definitely one of the most moving things I've ever experienced.

7
What the Fuck??

Nico and Darryl finished putting the barefooted sailor into a body bag. They labelled the bag and securely tied it to the diver's cage, which would be hoisted up to the ship, thirty-four metres above them. Then they returned to the wreck.

Control Room: *Okay, it looks like we're going down the stairs, alright, Nico?*

Nico gives the OK sign and starts crawling back onto the wreck. He enters through the open door and goes down a long passageway that he is now familiar with even in darkness — which is useful because there is zero visibility. He literally walks down the passageway without being able to see anything. At the end, he goes through a door to an area he hasn't been into before. The visibility here is also really poor, and he can't see anything.

Control Room: *If you put your hand on the wall and walk carefully forward... you can feel when you reach the corner.*

Nico gently places his glove on the wall and, by sliding his hand along it, he can follow the passageway, trying to avoid bumping into anything. He has to go slowly, partly to avoid stumbling over the equipment that lies where he's walking and partly to not overlook any possible bodies on the way. After a while, the passageway makes a ninety-degree turn.

Nico: *Yes, there's a corner here.*

Control Room: *Okay, go around the corner... wait... let me see... Sorry, it's quite difficult for us up here, we're trying to follow the ship's blueprints and guide you at the same time... hmm... okay, let me see...*
Nico: *I understand...*

Nico stands still and waits while Tony and the other diving managers on the ship try to make sense of the drawings depicting the three decks inside, filled with stairs, corners, cabins and passageways. All of which needs to be reversed when they instruct Nico.

Control Room: *Okay, so you've gone around the corner now?*

Nico grabs the wall and lets his hand slide around the corner, then continues through the murky waters.

Nico: *Yep.*

Slowly, Nico moves through the haze of sediment. His hand is still on the wall beside him.

Control Room: *So, you should see some stairs. You go down those stairs. Haven't you found the stairs yet?*
Nico: *Negative... Are the stairs towards the bow or the stern?*

Nico tries to look around. There's no sign of the typical stairwells on ships.

Control Room: *It should be right there... Can't you see anything?*
Nico: *There are no stairs down...*
Control Room: *You should be very close.*

Nico goes forward and sees a sign upside down. It says 'CAUTION — WATCH YOUR HEAD.'

Nico: *There's something here.*

Nico looks around but can't find any stairs. He looks down at the floor in front of him.

Control Room: *Remember, you're walking on the ceiling. The 'down' stairs will be above you.*

Nico turns and looks up. There's a chrome glinting in his light. He moves closer and sees that there are some narrow steps with chrome on the edges, continuing upwards in the darkness. In the control room, they watch through his helmet camera.

Control Room: *What do you have there? Those are stairs, right?*
Nico: *Yes. They're stairs... that's right.*
Control Room: *Okay, so you found them.*
Nico: *Yep.*
Control Room: *Okay, so now you need to go up them, alright?*
Nico: *Yep. I'm going up.*
Control Room: *Okay. Good. We're in the right place.*

In the images from Nico's helmet camera, you can see some steps, but at the same time, you can also see how little space there is on this kind of ship's staircase. It's almost a ladder, and there really isn't much room in the stairwell. Even without the heavy and large equipment, the thick umbilical and a diving tank on his back, the stairs would have been narrow. Nico has to squeeze up through the dark, compact stairwell by holding onto the railing and pulling himself upward.

Control Room: *Okay, how long are the stairs?... And how is the umbilical doing?... It's not getting caught in any corners or anything, right? Just be aware.*

Nico's umbilical is actually stuck on the railing and he must painstakingly back down and get it untangled before he can pull himself — backwards — up through the shaft. It's a very unpleasant and stressful journey for him.

Nico recounts, 'Even if I wanted to, I couldn't turn around. It was very tight, and as I pulled myself up, I could feel my umbilical getting pressed against the wall behind me. I had to squeeze myself up through the stairwell.'

> Midway up the stairwell, Nico has churned up so much sediment that visibility has completely disappeared again. It is as if he is standing in a bucket of grey paint. The image from his helmet camera shows only the white light as his lamp illuminates the sediment in front of it.
>
> **Control Room:** *Okay, so ... um ... are you on your way into the passageway now?*
>
> Nico emerges from the stairwell on all fours. He sits for a moment, catching his breath.
>
> **Control Room:** *Is that the floor I see there?*
>
> Nico breathes heavily.
>
> **Control Room:** *Eh? Are you okay, Nico?*
> **Nico:** *Uh ... I just need a moment to orientate myself.*
> **Control Room:** *Ah ... okay. No problem. Take your time.*
>
> The diving managers in the control room are all highly experienced, and they know that what Nico is doing is really demanding and completely outside the guidelines for what his type of diver usually does. They know that if Nico panics, they might not see him again, as, realistically, they won't be able to get him out of the wreck. So, they give him the break he needs. But they are not aware that Nico is at that moment about to 'go over the edge.' He has used up most of his energy, and he is far more affected than he sounds on the radio. It's as if it's dawning on him that what he's doing is really, really dangerous.
>
> Nico is now deeper into the wreck than ever before, and the journey up through the narrow stairwell has highlighted that if he makes a mistake here, there is no way out alive. The sensation of dragging

himself up through the tight stairwell—in the dark, where he could easily get stuck—spreads the feeling of claustrophobia inside him. It is one thing to pull yourself forward, upwards, deep into the 'nothingness' inside a sunken ship... But Nico knows that when he has to get out, it will all have to be done again, backwards, without any visibility in the too-narrow wreck.

If the murk had continued a bit longer, panic would have started to set in. With a bit of visibility, you can hope to find your way back to where you came from. But entirely without visibility, as the last part had been, it would have been almost impossible to get out. Of course, he could always navigate back along his umbilical to find the way which he'd come, but if he was completely blind it would still be impossible.

Fortunately, at the top of the stairs visibility is a little better. Now, on what would have been the deck below where he has just been, Nico sits, trying to orientate himself, breathing and preparing to continue.

Nico: *Uh... I think I am... at the top of the stairs now.*
Control Room: *All right, how are you doing, Nico? Are you okay?*
Nico: *Roger, I'm at the top of the stairs.*
Control Room: *Okay, so you're on the second floor now.*
Nico: *Roger. I'm on the second floor now.*
Control Room: *All right, and remember that you're walking on what used to be the ceiling.*
Nico: *Yeah, yeah...*
Control Room: *Okay.*

At that very moment, Nico feels something on his shoulder, and he instinctively jerks away.

Nico: *What the fuck??*

When I ask Nico what it was, he says — somewhat embarrassed — that it wasn't the first time he got a big fright inside the wreck. But here, in this situation, he felt something tap him on the shoulder and he flew to the other end of the room. He says he was actually very scared most of the time inside the dark wreck. When the bubbles disappeared, Nico could see again, and a somewhat clearer picture emerged on his camera — the outline of a dead man's hand appeared, floating in the water a little away from Nico.

Control Room: *What is it? Oh ... you found another one, yeah?*

The dead hand floats calmly in the water in front of Nico.

Control Room: *You found him in the passageway by the stairs, yeah?*

Nico reaches out to grab the hand and pull it towards him to wrestle the body out through the claustrophobic stairs and further out through the wreck.
    Then something very unexpected happens. The dead man ... takes hold of Nico's outstretched hand in the water.

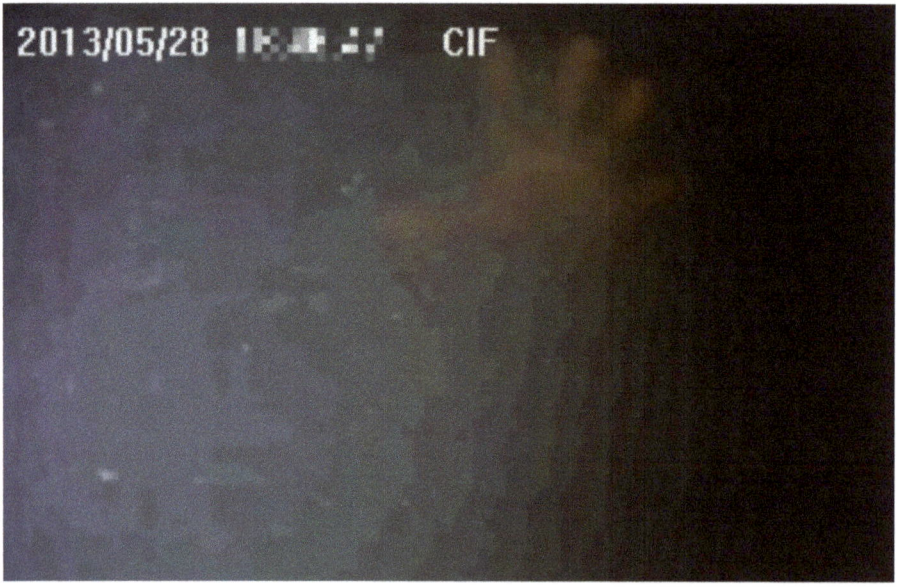

Authentic picture from Nico's camera.

8

I Have No Idea What to Do

At first, Nico tried to pull his hand away, but the dead man held on. Then Nico grabbed the hand.

Nico: *THERE'S SOMEONE ALIVE!!!*
Control Room: *HE'S ALIVE?? HE'S ALIVE??*
Nico: *He's alive????*

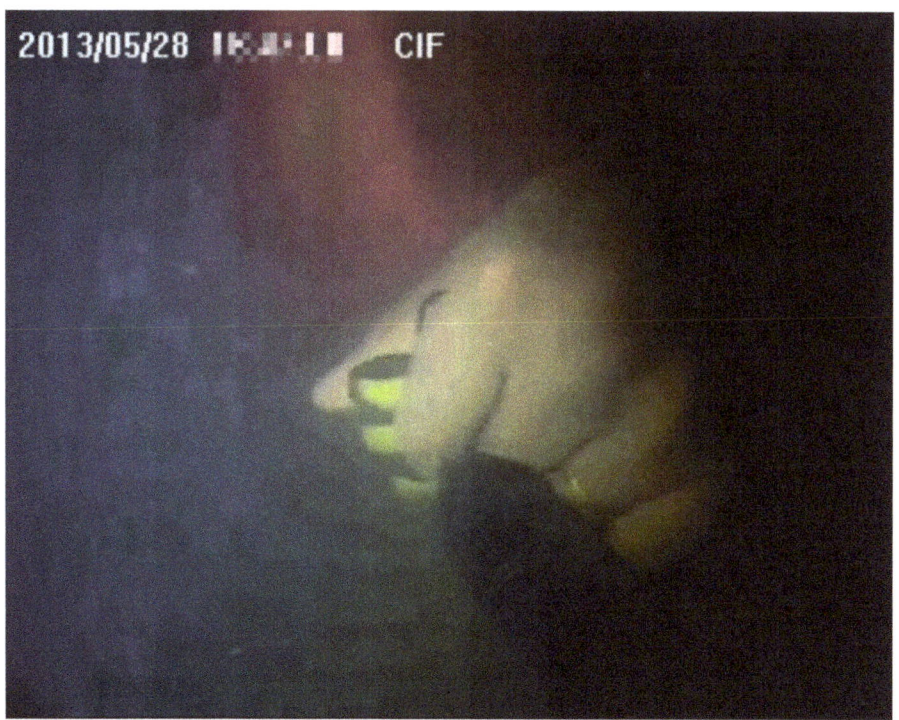

Authentic shot from Nico's helmet cam of Harrison's hand holding on.

Nico had no clue what was going on, but he could feel a hand tightly gripping his. The experience he'd just gone through with the dead sailors was so gruesome that suddenly feeling a hand's firm grip was incomprehensible and eerie.

'When I felt the hand grab mine, I thought it couldn't be real. It was impossible. The ship was underwater; it sank a long time ago… there couldn't be anyone alive underwater for that long. There was a bigger chance it was a zombie or something touching me. I got a big fright.'

Nico had no idea that there was an air pocket just above his head. There were thirty-four metres of water above them and everything on the wreck had been submerged for the last two days. So it was entirely incomprehensible to Nico that there could be a human being alive on the wreck. That couldn't be possible. But even though he was clueless, he kept holding on to the strange hand. And the hand he was holding did the same. But nobody knew what was going on. There was total chaos on the radio, as everyone shouted over each other.

Control Room: *Okay, make sure to hold onto him there… hold him there… just hold him, okay? Fuck, that was the last thing I expected.*

Up on the ship in dive control, they are just as confused. Nobody has yet understood that there must be an air pocket just above Nico's head. The only thing they can see in the pictures, and the only thing Nico can see, is a flooded wreck. How anyone can be alive there is something no-one can make sense of.

The otherwise calm and confident voice from dive control in Nico's radio now sounds anything but calm.

Control Room: *Stay there! I need to… We need to… What I need to do is… Okay…*
Nico: *What?… but… what… he's alive????*
Control Room: *All right, just keep holding onto him… hold him there, okay?*
Nico: *Roger.*

No-one had any idea what was going on. Still no-one could see anything other than a hand holding Nico's underwater. The hand squeezed Nico's until it suddenly let go and pulled away.

Harrison explains, 'When he grabbed my hand, I tried to pull him towards the side I came from because I was underwater, and I couldn't breathe. So eventually, I had to let go, so I could stand up and get air in the air pocket.'

This made Nico go after the hand and, to his great surprise, he broke through the water's surface in the flooded wreckage into a void — where an equally surprised Harrison stood watching him. Now Nico understood that there was an air pocket in the wreck, and a survivor was staring at him in shock. Nico looked back at him — just as shocked. Until now, Nico hadn't encountered a single pocket of air in the wreck, so no-one had thought it possible.

Authentic image from Nico's camera just as he discovers Harrison in the air pocket.

They look at each other for a while. Harrison is backed into a corner, still not entirely convinced that what is standing in front of him is, in fact, human.

Control Room: *Just be careful that he doesn't grab hold of you or anything like that.*

Nico tries to communicate with the frightened man. He is not sure if it's possible for the man to hear what he's trying to say through the thick metal of his diver's helmet. His voice is also a high-pitched Mickey Mouse style from the helium in the gas he is breathing.

Nico: *Hello. Stay there…Just stay there. Calm down.…just take it easy, my friend. Eaaasy, my friend. Easy. Just stay there.*

From the corner he's retreated into, Harrison looks at Nico in shock.

Control Room: *Stay there and give him a thumbs up, okay? And reassure him.*

Nico waves his arms in what is supposed to be a calming gesture.

Nico: *Everything is okay…Just stay there. Just step back a little…stay there.*

It's impossible to tell if it was having a calming effect. Both Nico and Harrison were equally shocked by the whole situation, and Harrison said a lot that Nico couldn't hear inside his large helmet.

'We were both scared. He kept telling me: "Go back, go in, go back," so I went back into the cabin so he wouldn't have to be scared…' Harrison recalls.

What had startled Nico in the water, just before he discovered what he thought was a dead man's hand, was Harrison tapping him on the shoulder. Harrison had been hearing something different in the shipwreck's many sounds for a while. He thought he had seen a kind of light reflection, but because of his severe oxygen deprivation and extreme fatigue, he thought it might be his imagination. Then he saw a mysterious light reflection in the water again, and actually became a bit frightened. He had previously heard sounds resembling a predator eating his dead comrades, and now something was approaching out of the dark wreck. Harrison was so exhausted that he wondered whether it was something supernatural coming to get him. When he became convinced that what he saw was not a figment of his imagination, he decided to go with it and face whatever was coming up the stairwell out of the darkness.

'I saw the reflection of some light. So, I looked … carefully … because I thought, "Is it a person … or is it something else? And if it's a person … I just don't want to miss it." So, I focused and looked at the light. The light intensified, and a bubble rose to the surface, so I kept looking until it reached the door to my cabin. I waited to see what would come out of the water. The light got brighter, but it was difficult to see what it was.'

At that time, Nico was still only on his way up the stairs, quite a distance from where Harrison was located. So, the only thing Harrison saw was an occasional flicker of light.

'For the time I had been trapped in the wreck, I hadn't seen any light or reflection or anything. So, when I saw the light, I could not be sure it was a person. But when I saw the helmet, I thought it could be a person. But the next thing that occurred to me was, "How do I make him aware that I'm here?" He was still far away and might swim in another direction.'

Harrison stepped down from the makeshift platform that kept him above the water and approached the place where the stairs descended into the small passageway outside his cabin. There was no air pocket here since the ship was tilted, so if he wanted to get closer to the light, he had to put his head back underwater.

Harrison recalls the tension of that moment, 'I had to approach him cautiously. I dived underwater and swam to him. But he didn't see me. He was moving away again, so I had to reach out to him underwater. But I knew he would be startled by being touched because there's no-one in his situation who wouldn't be scared, so I just tapped him lightly on the shoulder and kept away from him.'

That's what Nico felt before he discovered Harrison's hand. And, as Harrison had anticipated, Nico was spooked and flew to the other end of the pitch-black room.

'He moved very fast. He was very scared. But there was no way out where he was going. He ended up in the corner of the cabin. So, he was just there.'

Nico remembers it well, 'I thought I would... It felt like I was about to faint... [laughing]... I can't put into words the emotions that went through me when it happened... it was *so* wild... I was extremely startled.'

Harrison could barely hold his breath any longer and had to return to the air pocket, but he was nervous that the diver, or whatever it was, would disappear. So, he reached his hand down as far towards the light as he could, in the direction he had seen the diver.

'I waved my hands to him to let him know that I was alive. I wasn't sure if he saw me... So, I reached my hand out so he could see me.'

And that's how Nico discovered the hand which he initially thought belonged to another dead sailor. If Nico had been just a few metres further away, Harrison might not have succeeded in making contact with him, and the diver would have disappeared elsewhere on the wreck.

Nico is still moved when he recounts what happened.

Tony remembers the mood in the dive control room: 'It slowly dawned on all of us that... there was a survivor. There was someone alive in there.

Miracles do happen.'

But Nico suddenly appearing in Harrison's air pocket was overwhelming for Harrison, and he retreated to the farthest corner until he fully understood his own incredible luck. He simply couldn't believe that a diver had really come into the innermost part of the wreck to save him. How could that happen? No divers he had ever heard of could do that. Where did he come from?

> **Control Room:** *Okay, just reassure him, pat him on the shoulder. Just tell him to relax. We're here to help, tell him… uh… just keep reassuring him all the time.*
>
> **Nico:** *Roger, Roger.*

Nico makes reassuring gestures to Harrison and tries to give him a comforting smile through the small window in the helmet.

> **Nico:** [To Harrison] *Just relax, my friend. Just relax.*

Harrison just stands there, looking at Nico. He still doesn't fully comprehend that there is indeed a real diver.

> **Control Room:** [More or less to themselves]… *Fucking hell. I have no idea what we should do.* [To Nico] *Just keep him there, keep him calm, okay?*

Dive control isn't the only one unsure of what to do. Neither Nico nor Harrison takes any action. They just stand there, looking at each other. Nobody had imagined this in their wildest dreams.

Nico tried to look reassuring, but he honestly didn't know what he was going to do with Harrison. It would probably have been difficult to wrestle a body out of that space, but it might *just* be possible. With a living person though, things are different. It's simply not possible — not in any conceivable way. It's not like you can bend the rules or come up with a clever way to do it. It is — without exaggeration — simply impossible to get a person out alive from there. That's it.

Nico tried once again to appear reassuring to the man standing, desperate, in the corner of the small cabin. The man apparently believed that he was now saved. But Nico had no idea what to do.

'Immediately, all these emotions started rushing up, and you begin to think about different scenarios, and what will you do, how is it possible, how do we get him out? This just can't be right … It was completely, utterly overwhelming; there is a lot going through your mind in such a situation.'

While Nico stood there, trying to show Harrison that everything was under control, the exact opposite was happening in his radio communication from dive control, which normally remained super calm and was never shaken, no matter what happened.

> **Control Room:** *Fuck, I didn't expect that, did you?*
> **Nico:** *Absolutely wild…*
> **Control Room:** *Did you get a fright?*
> **Nico:** *Yes!! Holy cow!*
> **Control Room:** *I got a fright when he started grabbing your hand.*
> **Nico:** *Me too … wow …*
> **Control Room:** *Damn incredible. For fuck's sake …*

This was a funny part of the interviews because everyone who had experienced it laughed spontaneously whenever we got to this part of the story. Even though we had been through it many times before.

Tony chuckled as he recalled it, 'I mean, everyone was shocked because at that point, everyone had given up hope of finding anyone alive. He was obviously shocked because he had been found. And we were shocked because we found someone.'

> Inside the wreck, Nico is still trying to reassure Harrison. Harrison has come to terms with the fact that it is a diver and that there is nothing to be nervous about. He steps forward a bit towards Nico.

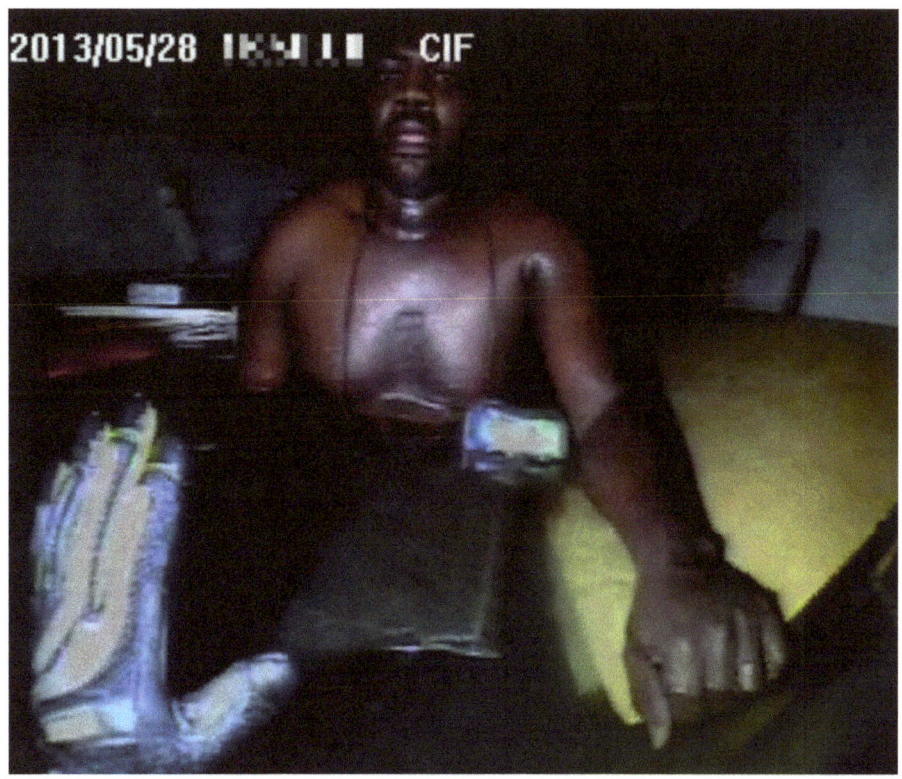

Authentic image from Nico's helmet camera in the air pocket deep inside the wreck.

Control Room: *Uh, how should we talk to him? Try to check if he can hear you. Ask him if there are any other survivors.*

With a mix of sign language and speaking very loudly and clearly in his diver helmet, Nico tries to communicate with Harrison.

Nico: *Are there any other survivors?*

It takes a moment before Harrison realizes Nico is talking to him. Then he understands and responds, also with a mix of sign language and by speaking as loudly and clearly as his lack of oxygen allows. He says something and waves his hand defensively.

Nico: *None? Only you? None?*
Control Room: *No others at all?*
Nico: *Roger...*

Harrison explains something to Nico.

Nico: *He says he has heard some shouting for a while. But now it has been silent for a long time.*
Control Room: *Okay. Understood. I think he had the largest air pocket; that's why. Okay, first, we need to get him some water and some food. Ask him if he's thirsty.*
Nico: *Are you thirsty?*

Harrison shakes his head.

Control Room: *Okay. Okay, he apparently had a Sprite. There's a Sprite floating there, okay?*
Control Room: *Alright. Ask him if he's hungry.*
Nico: *Are you hungry?*

Harrison shakes his head. He doesn't understand why they don't just rescue him, but he's too tired to ask. He can hardly breathe and just wishes they would quickly get him out of the flooded cabin.

Control Room: *He's not hungry either. He's okay. Just tell him to relax; we'll help him. Just keep reassuring him all the time.*
Nico: *Roger.* [To Harrison] *Just relax, my friend.*
Control Room: *Give him a thumbs up, okay?*

Nico gives Harrison a thumbs up. Harrison nods, knowing he is saved. In a very short time he will be able to breathe freely again and will be back on land. Far away from this horrible place.

What Harrison didn't know is that unfortunately, he couldn't have been more wrong. Neither Nico nor dive control had the faintest idea of how in the world they could get him out of there. That's why they hadn't taken any action yet. He was by no means saved; he would by no means be able to breathe soon; and it was by no means certain that he would leave this place alive. In fact, no-one was entirely sure where exactly the air pocket was.

> **Control Room:** *Do you have any idea of exactly where on the ship you are? Where do you think you are? When you came in from the stairs, where were you? Look around, let us see where we are, so we can find out if we can get him out.*
>
> Nico tries to orientate himself and looks for other exits underwater. But it does not help him very much.

Nico was perplexed: 'Immediately, you start thinking: "How do we get this person out of here? We are deep inside the wreck — underwater." I didn't even know exactly where I was... I couldn't see how we would manage it. If we tried to get him out he would most likely die from it, and then I'd have killed the man who thought I was there to save him. It felt really uncomfortable.'

9

How the Hell Do We Get Him Out

Dive control had finally identified where on the wreck Harrison was trapped. Unfortunately, it was not encouraging. He was almost as far inside as it was possible to be and the way out was full of obstacles.

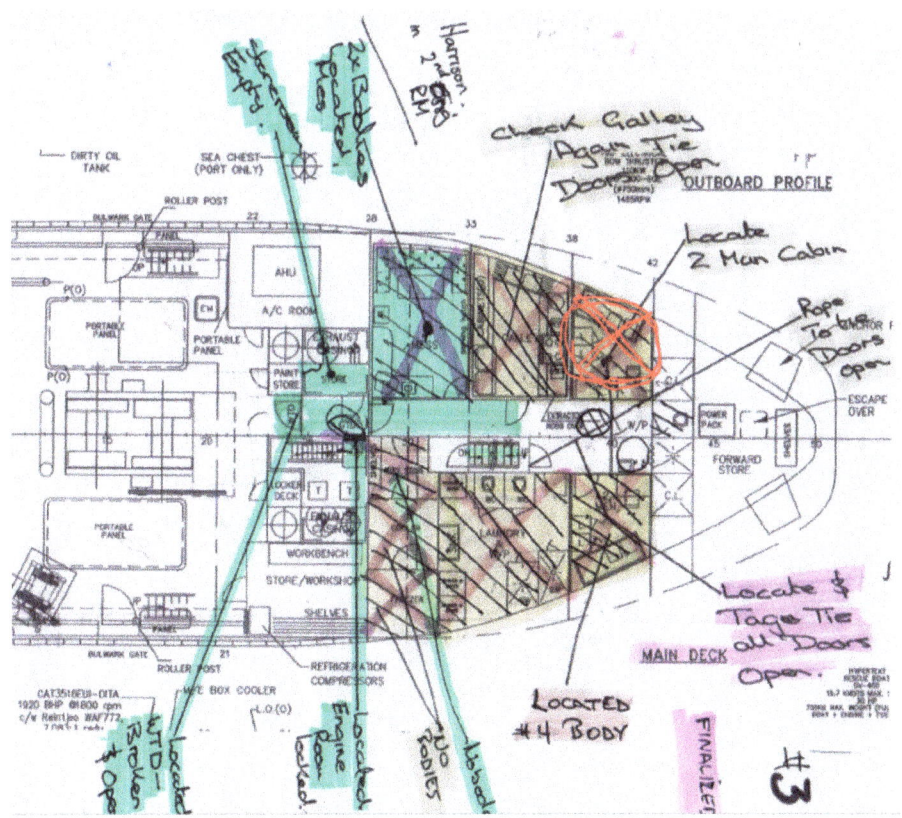

The cabin Harrison was in, top-right, marked with a red X in a circle on the *Jascon 4* plan that the dive team were using.

Nico remembers what was going through his mind, 'I thought, "What do we do now? I mean, I'm in full diving gear and can breathe underwater. I'm in a wetsuit, I have a helmet on my head and lights. I'm fine. But him... he's sitting there in his underwear, deep inside this wreck — underwater. So how do we... I mean... what do we do?" Immediately, all those things start racing through your head. "How the hell do we get him out?" I mean, "What's the plan?"'

It was not surprising that Nico felt that way, because *there was no plan*. And no realistic possibility of making a plan. Harrison was in a place where he just couldn't easily get out.

Tony explains, 'Finding him is one thing. But from there... once you find him, you have to make a plan to get him out safely. Finding him was the least of the two problems...'

Harrison had been down there so long that even if they could rescue him, he would most likely die. Tony summed up the realities.

'All the stairs and passageways and doors on the vessel are very narrow. Not much more than a narrow door in width. You have different levels and floors, stairs that go up, which are actually stairs that go down, and vice versa, and a lot of door openings to go through. It would be very difficult to get him out. Especially so far and so deep inside the wreck. He was right in the furthest part... as deep down as you can get.

'He was in a cabin — far inside, up some narrow stairs. From there, you have to get him all the way out — underwater. And then you have to get him from the wreck into the diving bell. And then you have to bring him up to the diving vessel and into the diving system in a pressure chamber because he can't go directly to the surface. The time he had been underwater... about sixty-two hours... would surely give him the bends if he went straight up from there. I mean, he had been three whole days underwater... that's really a long time. He would die instantly if we tried to get him up.'

Dive control knew it. Nico knew it. They knew that there was no realistic way to save Harrison. But it was Nico who was face-to-face with Harrison down on the wreck... and Harrison didn't know any of that. On the contrary, he was sure he was saved the moment he saw Nico and grabbed his hand. But what actually went through Harrison's head when he stood there with Nico?

'I was so excited to get out of the wreck. And happy. That was the only thing in my head: "You are going out, you are going out, you are going out."'

Nico, though, thought otherwise: 'I was stressed because we had to come up with a plan to get him out. Quickly. I felt there was a lot of pressure on me to ensure that we got the best possible result. And unfortunately, there weren't really any ideas on how we should approach it.'

This is a delicate way of saying that everyone, of course, would do what they could, but Harrison's odds were really bad. One of the things that made an impression on Nico was something he noticed when Harrison grabbed his hand underwater.

'I could see the wedding ring on his finger, so you knew he was a family man. I had this person's life in my hands. It was up to us to ensure that he survived, that he got out of this wreck and saw his family again. It was my responsibility.'

Of course, everyone would do everything they could to rescue Harrison, but these were professional people who all knew that there was no emergency procedure to cover a situation like this one.

Nico continues, 'We *had* to come up with a plan to get him out. But at the same time, I knew that there was an imminent chance that this plan would kill the man it was supposed to save. Getting him out would be life-threatening — no matter what we came up with.'

It looked bleak. No standard procedure could be used to save Harrison and they hadn't yet come up with any other plan. But there was no reason to let Harrison know that. Not yet. Nico signalled to Harrison in the flooded cabin.

Nico: *Just relax, stay calm. We'll get you out.*

Harrison nods.

Control Room: *Is he calming down?*
Nico: *Yes, he's calm now.*

Nico smiles at Harrison as convincingly as he can.

Tony sums it up: 'At this point, we didn't expect to find anyone alive after so much time underwater. And the fact that we did — it posed a big problem for us.'

Up on the diving vessel, Tony and everyone else frantically tried to come up with a plan. The radio was on, so Nico could hear everything they were saying while he tried to reassure Harrison that he was safe. Fortunately, Harrison couldn't hear what Nico could.

> **Control Room:** *Okay… okay… Damn, man… We need to find a way to get him to the surface… Damn… Fuck, this is going to be hard… I don't know what to do.*

When I asked Tony if it's really that difficult to get a man up from a depth of thirty-four metres, he looked completely bewildered.

'Of course, it was a massive problem. Massive! Clearly, it would be very hard to get him out of the wreck… because he was so deep inside the wreck… A big problem. There was a mountain of work ahead of us if it was going to succeed.'

Nico had now been inside Harrison's flooded cabin for a good long while. He was still trying to make it look like they knew what they were doing and that everything was under control. Contrary to reality. There was, unusually, great confusion in Nico's radio from his colleagues up in dive control.

> **Control Room:** *Um… We have, uh… What about…? That we have… well, no, that won't work… what about a long air hose from… uh… no… that won't work… he's under pressure…*

'In the beginning, there was simply no plan to get him out. We couldn't think of anything. No plan at all,' Tony admitted.

When Nico talks about what was going on, you can tell that he didn't like it at all: 'I sat there on the bottom, looking at Harrison, while I could hear the conversations in dive control. I wondered what he was thinking.'

Harrison divulges, 'The diver sitting in front of me, of course, couldn't know it, but inside me, there were a lot of tears of joy because I thought, "Finally, God has heard my prayers and I'm saved, I'm going to get out of this place after all this time… all the time I've spent here thinking I'm going to die." To be in there, to see the water filling the whole ship and experience it sinking… the darkness and everything, and now I'm going to be alive. I was so, so excited and happy inside ... now I was going back to see my family. I thought I was going out, and then I would be taken directly home to my family.'

Unfortunately, up in dive control, Tony and the others hadn't come any closer to a solution.

> **Control Room:** *Uh ... maybe we could take ... I mean, from the diving bell ... we could take, hmm ... take an umbilical from there into ... no, for fuck's sake, that won't work ...*

'I sat there looking at Harrison while I could hear all the confused voices on the radio from dive control. It wasn't particularly comforting.' Nico explains.

Tony can imagine his diver's predicament, but only in retrospect: 'All the time Nico was with Harrison he didn't know what to do to get him out. And unfortunately, we didn't have time to think about Nico, who sat there not knowing what to say to the poor man down there who thought he was saved ... but who probably began to wonder why we didn't get him out soon ... we didn't think about that. We were too busy. It probably wasn't very nice for Nico.'

At that time, the team used what is called an open circuit on the radio system between divers and dive control, diving bell and technicians. This meant that everyone could listen to all communication throughout. These events actually contributed to changing this practice. It clearly wasn't an advantage for Nico to hear how confused they were in the control room.

There was a lot of communication going back and forth, and they called experts on land, but since no-one had ever found a survivor on a wreck who had survived for three days at this kind of depth, there was no immediate solution.

It must have been extremely uncomfortable for Nico to be the intermediary. He was the one looking Harrison in the eye, while in his radio he could hear one solution after another being rejected.

> **Control Room:** *No, that won't work ... What are you saying? ... Yeah, but he's under pressure. We still have ... no ... we don't ... What do you mean? — Ah? No ... we can't ... no ... no ...*

'We didn't have time to say much to Nico, but he was smart enough to keep Harrison calm. He gave Harrison the impression that everyone knew what we would do to save him,' explains Tony.

Nico describes what it was like for him, 'It wasn't particularly reassuring... I could hear one guy in control saying one thing, and another guy saying something else, and dive control answering, "How the hell... What, oh no... it can't be done... blah, blah, blah."'

Meanwhile, Nico stood there nodding kindly to Harrison while listening to the arguments on the radio.

> **Control Room:** *Remember: Decompression! He's been at a depth of thirty-four metres... for... for three days, for fuck's sake!*

Nico continues, 'If someone comes to save you, you want to see *confidence* in that person's eyes. This person is here to save me! You don't want to hear that guy say: "Hmmm... Let's see what we can do... oh no... For fuck's sake, we actually don't know what to do." So, I did what I could to look as professional as possible, so he could feel comfortable and believe that we knew what we were doing. So, he believed that we could actually save him.'

> It is at this point that they begin to truly notice Harrison's condition for the first time. He is now completely pale and breathing very heavily. There has been so much to think about since they discovered him, that no-one has thought much about the state he is in. Now everyone's eyes are suddenly focused on Harrison. He sits as he did before Nico appeared, labouring to breathe.
>
> **Control Room:** *Actually, is he breathing okay? Is he struggling to breathe, you think?*
> **Nico:** *Yeah, he's struggling. Quite a lot.*
> **Control Room:** *Okay. Not good.*

'I couldn't breathe very well anymore. The oxygen was about to disappear completely. I was fighting for air.' Harrison recalls.

Tony could see the problem, 'At that point, he began to breathe very heavily, which was a result of the oxygen contamination in the air pocket he was in. That is... the oxygen was simply running out.'

Nico was considering what he could do: 'As a saturation diver, your respiratory system is closed. It's not like recreational divers who can share air from their tanks. We can't. Everything is enclosed in the cables. But you can open a valve to purge the system by releasing gas. And I thought to myself, "If I release gas in here in the air pocket, he will at least have some fresh oxygen." But the mixture I was breathing was helium and oxygen, and I didn't know how the helium in the mixture would affect his body. It could easily be dangerous for him because there are a lot of scientific things going on inside his body due to the time he's been submerged. But I didn't know enough about it.'

As part of what Nico breathed in was helium, that was obviously something completely different from the normal atmospheric air that Harrison had been breathing inside the wreck. Nico looked at Harrison, who was breathing in a strained and gasping kind of way.

> **Nico:** *Can I let out a bit of gas for him? Should I give him something from my helmet?*
> **Control Room:** *No, we can't. It's helium! We can't... let's not rush this... Remember, how long has he been in there... let me see... for sixty-two hours... Shit... poor man...*

> Up in dive control, there's a lot of talking back and forth. There's some background chatter, and others are chiming in.

> **Control Room:** *Well? Yeah, okay... No, that won't work either...* [talking to others up there] *Go and have a meeting on the bridge and contact some diving doctors on land... let's figure out if we can get him out.*

Tony explains their dilemma: 'Clearly, there was a lot of communication back and forth with experts on land. And a lot of input from different people. Unfortunately, they couldn't really help. They knew a lot about what *not* to do... but there was no-one who had experience with this... we always work according to a protocol, with things that have been tested a thousand times... but this... no-one had experienced this before.'

Since there were no precedents for Harrison's situation, no-one knew what would happen if they gave him helium. But it was straightforward to figure out what would happen if they didn't do it. Harrison wouldn't have lasted much longer without fresh air. Nico had to provide it.

'Eventually, I was told to open the valve on my helmet and release helium and oxygen so he could get some fresh air. We just had to hope that his body could tolerate it.'

Control Room: *Okay, we have to try... okay? Nico? Let some gas into the cabin, just to give him a little oxygen, okay? Then we'll see if it harms him.*

Nico opens the valve in his helmet and it doesn't take long to fill the small space with helium and oxygen.

Control Room: *All right, stop.*

Nico closes the valve and looks at Harrison attentively. Now the small air pocket is filled with a mixture of helium and oxygen, and if Harrison can't tolerate helium inside his pressurized body, he will lose consciousness in the next few moments.

In dive control, everyone moves closer to the monitor showing the image from Nico's helmet camera. On the screen, they can see a grainy image of Harrison struggling to breathe.

Control Room:... *Does it seem like he's breathing better now?*

Nico moves a bit closer to Harrison.

Nico: *Yes... he looks okay... or better...*

Harrison eagerly inhales air into his lungs for the first time in many hours.

'It felt *so* good to be able to breathe again. It was as if I suddenly woke up from a dream. I could suddenly see clearly again and felt... maybe not good... but at least much better.'

Nico shared some of his relief, but the bigger picture weighed on his mind: 'It was good that he got a bit more air... but we still had to get him out. He had already been dangerously long under pressure. The obvious option — or the only option — was to get him out. But there aren't many ways to do that.'

Tony wasn't optimistic, 'Of course, we couldn't bring him to the surface right away... he had to decompress for a very long time first... and that was impossible. The bends would, like I said, kill him. So, what should we do?'

Nico just wanted to know what was going to happen, 'I was very stressed about what decision was made to get him out. After all, it was me who had to do it...'

10

The Plan

Harrison later told me: 'I wasn't really aware of what was going on. I didn't understand what we were waiting for. I just wanted out of the wreckage as quickly as possible and home to my family.'

After debating for more than an hour and turning the problem over to the experts ashore over the radio, dive control ended up with the best possible plan, given the circumstances. Or maybe it's pushing it too far to call it a plan … It certainly wasn't a surefire way to get Harrison out, but it was — as far as they could tell — probably the only way.

No help could come from the diving ship or from anywhere else — it was either impossible or would take too long. They had to get Harrison up as soon as possible. Dive control had to put a plan into action using only the three divers underwater: Nico, inside the wreck with Harrison; Darryl, outside it; and André, in the diving bell. They would have to carry out the plan. Alone.

Control Room: *Okay… Now we have a plan. Here's what we're going to do guys, are you all listening?*
Nico: *Roger.*
Control Room: *And, Darryl, are you with me?*
Darryl: *Yeah, Roger, mate.*
Control Room: *Darryl? You are outside the wreck. So, you have to go get André's diving helmet over in the diving bell, okay?*
Darryl: *Roger.*
Control Room: *You're a backup diver, Darryl… so you can't walk in on Nico with the helmet. You have to stay outside the wreckage and look after Nico's umbilical… So, Nico?*
Nico: *Yes. I'm here…*

> **Control Room:** *You'll need to get to Darryl outside the wreckage and get André's diving helmet from Darryl. And then you take it in the wreckage to the survivor, Nico. And then we slowly lead him out with the helmet on.*
>
> **Nico:** *Okay. Understood.*

That was the plan, in all its simplicity: they would give Harrison a spare diving helmet to wear — so that he would be able to breathe — and Nico would guide him out of the wreck.

It doesn't sound like a strategy that should have taken many hours to come up with, but there's a reason it wasn't straightforward. First, it is not as simple as it sounds; and secondly, nobody knew how Harrison's body would react, or if he would even be able to dive. The only diving equipment he would use was a heavy, technically complicated helmet, and he had most likely never dived before. There were many things that could complicate the execution of the plan, and getting all the way out through the narrow wreck was life-threatening, even for a trained diver like Nico. Given that, how would it go with a completely inexperienced, totally exhausted and untested person, with no diving equipment other than a helmet? It was almost bound to go wrong. But it was the only option they had.

> **Control Room:** *Darryl, you're going to have to watch both your umbilicals and help Nico get the survivor back to the basket, okay?*

Giving Harrison a spare diving helmet meant that he also had to get air via one of the thick unwieldy umbilicals. For the plan to succeed, safety diver Darryl would need to remain outside the wreck, where he'd continue pulling Nico's cable in and out while now also managing Harrison's umbilical as well. That may not sound like a particularly difficult task, but it is. With Nico so far inside the wreck, it had required Darryl's full attention just to control one umbilical as it travelled around corners and up and down stairs. It was very difficult to pull it out and in — and it was incredibly heavy. Now Darryl had to control two of those intractable umbilicals — alone.

> **Darryl:** *Okay. I'm ready.*

Another problem with giving Harrison the spare diving helmet was that *there is no spare diving helmet* in a sat diving team. The third helmet belonged to André, monitoring air supply and technical details inside the diving bell. He was not wearing his helmet because there is air inside a bell — but it was his helmet they planned to lend to Harrison. First, they had to get hold of it from André.

Control Room: *Okay, in the bell?? Hello?... André?*

On the camera hanging from the ceiling in the diving bell, you can see that André has fallen asleep. It may seem sloppy, but there is not much to do in the tiny room, and no-one has contacted him for many hours.

Control Room: *André! Wake up! André!*
André: [Awakening] *What?... Sorry.*

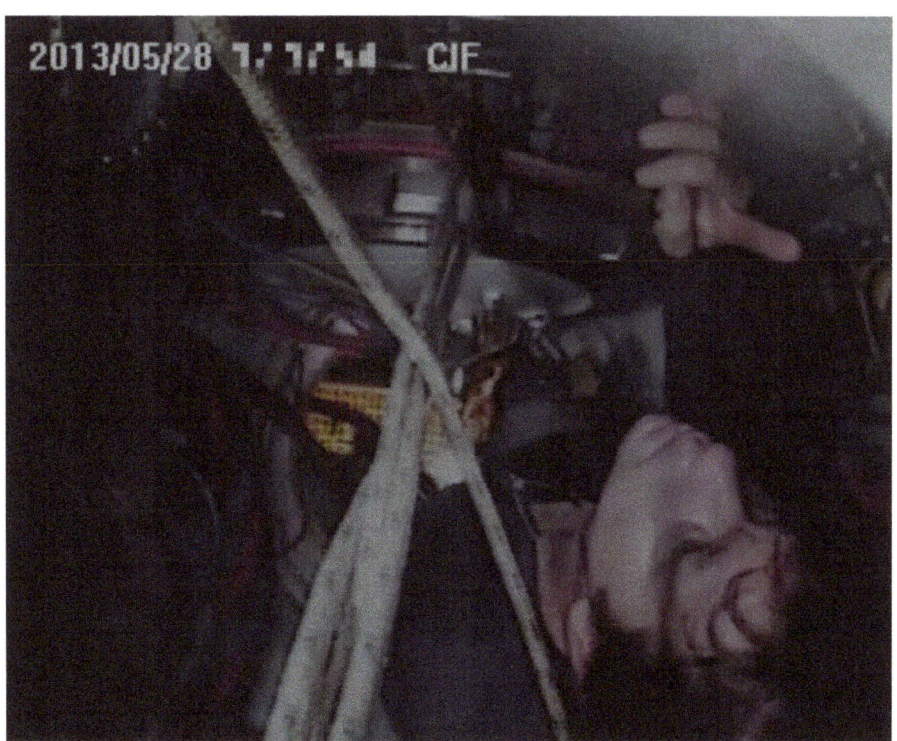

Authentic picture of André inside the diving bell.

Control Room: *Okay, here's what happened: we found a survivor.*
André: *You have found a what??*
Control Room: *We found a survivor, okay?*
André: *What?... Okay.*
Control Room: *So, what's going to happen is: We're going to have you unlock your helmet out of the system and hand it out of the bell to Darryl, who then takes it to Nico, who brings it into the survivor, okay?*
André: *Understood.*

André quickly starts to get the helmet ready and turns on its air supply.

Control Room: *So, Darryl?*
Darryl: *Yeah?*
Control Room: *André is sticking his helmet out under the bell now, okay? Get to the bell and grab it.*

Darryl now has to let Nico's thick umbilical tend itself and move all the way over to the diving bell, where André lowers his diving helmet through the hatch at the bottom. From this moment André can no longer get out to help the other two divers. If something happens, he has no way to save himself—or the others, because his helmet and air supply is now on its way deep into the wreck. If anything happens to the bell or the air supply, he'll drown immediately.
   Darryl arrives at the bell and grabs André's diving helmet.

Control Room: *Okay. Cool. And then it has to go to the wreck so Nico can get it into the survivor. He will meet you at the door.*

Darryl starts unrolling the hose that will give Harrison air inside André's helmet.

Control Room: *Alright. Hello in the bell again? André? Now I want you to find a bottle of water and hand it to Darryl, okay?*
André: *A bottle of water?*

Control Room: *Yep. A bottle of water. The survivor needs something to drink.*

Inside the bell, André finds a water bottle in his bag.

Control Room: *It's full, right?*
André: *Yep.*
Control Room: *Okay, brilliant... let's get it in to him.*

André hands the water out through the hatch at the bottom of the bell to Darryl, who now has a bottle, a diving helmet and a long air hose to keep track of. These items and a body harness that will hold the helmet and attach it to the unwieldy umbilical, will all need to go in to Harrison. The easiest thing would be for Darryl to crawl into the wreck with them. But Harrison is too deep inside the wreckage. It is absolutely impossible for Darryl to crawl all the way in, as there is no-one outside to tend the three umbilicals: Darryl's own, Nico's and the new one for Harrison. The umbilicals would soon get stuck and as André now has no helmet he cannot get out of the diving bell to help. The only one who can get the equipment to Harrison is Nico.

Control Room: *Okay, Nico?*
Nico: *Yes, Roger?*
Control Room: *Nico, now we have André's helmet and umbilical.*
Nico: *Roger.*
Control Room: *So, Nico, you're going to have to come all the way out of the wreck and get it.*
Nico: *Yes. Okay.*

The plan was for Nico to crawl all the way to the outermost doorway and get the items from Darryl, who would then be in charge of all three umbilicals. But to carry out the plan, Nico had to leave Harrison, and when he did, all light in the small room disappeared. Harrison would once again be left alone in total darkness.

Nico later told me, 'It felt awful leaving him there. If I was in his situation and someone was there to save me, I wouldn't want that person to leave. If he went, I would go with him.'

> **Control Room:** *Okay Nico, now Darryl is coming back to the wreck. You'll have to get out of the wreckage and get the helmet and the water... okay?*

Nico recalls how concerned he was at that critical moment: 'It didn't feel right. I wanted to make sure he didn't try to swim with me first. He wouldn't survive that.'

> Before Nico leaves, he tries to explain that Harrison should just take it easy and stay where he is. Nico is nervous about how much Harrison can hear through the big helmet.
>
> **Nico:** [To Harrison] *Don't worry my friend. Do not worry.*
> **Control Room:** *What is it?*
> **Nico:** *I'm just telling him to keep calm.*
> **Control Room:** *Why?... Did he get out of control?*
> **Nico:** *No it's just... I'll tell him I'll be back.*
> **Control Room:** *Well? Okay, okay.*
> **Nico:** [To Harrison] *Stay there! I go down, I come back. Okay? Stay there.*

'When he left me, he said to me, "Don't worry. I'll be back, don't worry, I'll be back." But I wasn't afraid at all anymore, because I'd already made up my mind: "If this is death, let it come. If I survive, I survive."' Harrison later told me.

> Nico gives Harrison a 'thumbs up' and dives into the pitch-black water. For a short while, Nico's lamp still illuminates the cabin underwater, but as Nico crawls out through the wreckage, all light disappears and the cramped cabin is pitch-black again. It gets quiet and Harrison is alone once more.

The trip out through the wreckage is not easy for Nico. It is a long way and he has to do part of it backwards, because his umbilical is so stiff that he cannot turn around in the narrow passages. He knows that, in a little while, he will have to make the same trip — all the way back into the wreck — and next time, he will not only have his own cumbersome umbilical trailing behind him, he will have two: his own and Harrison's.

After quite a while, Nico's lamp appears in the dark corridor leading to the outermost door.

Control Room: *Okay Darryl, are you ready for Nico to come out in a bit?*
Darryl: *Roger, I'm at the door.*

Reconstruction: Darryl outside the wreck.

Control Room: *Okay, okay. Nico, go to the door... and get the helmet and the water, right?*
Nico: *Roger. I'm working on it... I'm almost there.*

When, with great difficulty, Nico finally crawls out through the wreckage and reaches the door, he is handed the spare helmet with its long stiff umbilical and a bottle of water and then has to head back through the dark wreckage.

Control Room: *Okay, do you have water, Nico? All right, give him the helmet, Darryl.*
Darryl: *Check.*
Control Room: *Excellent. Take it to the survivor, we don't want to spend too much time away from him as long as he's sitting all alone in the dark.*
Nico: *Copy, copy.*
Control Room: *Good job guys.*

So far, everything was going to plan. But they had neglected to consider one very important detail, one which you might think was completely obvious… but which, for a sat diver, is easily overlooked.

11

The Cook Always Survives

Nico was on his way to Harrison, deep inside the wreckage: 'I had to go all the way down the hall ... into the room before the stairs ... find the stairs, squeeze myself and all my equipment up the stairs ... walk through the small hallway after the stairs, walk across the small living room with various doors, enter through one of them, and then into a very unpleasant room that lay to the side, and then I had to get the harness and the helmet mounted on him.'

In order to get the diving helmet to sit firmly on Harrison's head — and to stay on someone wearing only a pair of underpants — Nico had brought a harness, something like the sort of device that mountain climbers use. Harrison had to wear this to provide the helmet and the air hose something to attach to.

'When Nico came back, he gave me the harness to put on. I hadn't seen a harness like that before, so I had no idea what to do. I tried to put it on, but I couldn't figure it out. Also, my legs were so exhausted from standing up for almost three days that I had no control over them. I was confused and didn't know what to do, so the diver helped me. But I just thought, "Um, why am I wearing this strange harness?" Until I saw the hat ... the diving helmet. Then I understood that they could really save me, because if I put on the hat, I could breathe properly, just like the diver ... also underwater.'

> **Control Room:** *Okay let's ... let's get that helmet on his head so we can reduce CO2, please.*
>
> Nico quickly begins the process of putting the helmet onto Harrison. Like the other diving helmets, it has radio communication so dive

control can talk to the person wearing it. As soon as Harrison gets the helmet down over his head, he can breathe properly.

Control Room: [To Harrison] *Hello my friend, can you hear me?*
Harrison: *Yes, I can.*
Control Room: *Okay, listen to me. We'll put the helmet on so you can breathe, okay?*
Harrison: *Yes, sir!*

Harrison had never dived before, especially not with a huge and complicated diving helmet like this.

'It felt quite uncomfortable ... it's a very claustrophobic feeling, but for me right there ... then it was wonderful! And when I had the hat on, I was *so* comfortable. The breathing air was *so* good. I felt really good.'

Control Room: *Okay, now don't panic, okay? You have to listen to me, okay? I want you to stay calm, okay? Are you okay?*
Harrison: *Yes, sir!*
Control Room: *Have you any injuries?*
Harrison: *No, sir, no injuries.*
Control Room: *Okay. What's your name?*
Harrison: *Harrison. Harrison.*
Control Room: *Okay, Harrison. Now we'll get you home, okay?*
Harrison: *Thank you, Sir!*
Control Room: *The diver helping you now, his name is Nico.*
Harrison: *Okay ... Nico.*

But Harrison still didn't know what was going to happen: 'I had no idea what they were up to. But I didn't actually wonder about it either. I was just happy to wear that hat. When they put the hat on me, he said on the radio in the helmet, "Are you okay?" I said, "Yes." When he told me Nico's name that, "There is the diver Nico, he wants to take you from that place," I was very, very happy. He seemed nice, the diver. I wasn't thinking about what was going to happen, I was just completely excited that I was going to be out of the wreckage soon.'

Harrison was happy. But he didn't know how dangerous a trip he was about to embark on. And there was no reason to tell him. It would probably dawn on him soon enough, anyway. Right then, it was just a matter of making sure there wouldn't be any surprises.

Control Room: *Nico, say hello.*
Nico: *Hey Harrison, can you hear me?*
Harrison: *Yes!*

Nico gives Harrison the thumbs up.

Nico: *You have to keep calm, right?*
Harrison: *Yes, sir!*
Control Room: *So, we have Nico here fixing your helmet, okay? There is another diver outside. His name is Darryl. He'll help you too, okay?*
Harrison: *Yes.*

Nico recalls Harrison's demeanour: 'He was extremely compliant. I think at that point he was so overwhelmed by the situation he was in that he basically closed his eyes and put his life in our hands.'

Inhaling a mixture of helium and oxygen, as sat divers do and as Harrison was then also doing, changes your voice — it gives you that characteristic Mickey Mouse sound — which makes it difficult for the inexperienced to understand what is being said. Even the experienced can find it difficult.

Control Room: *Harrison? What is your full name?*
Harrison: *Okene Harrison.*
Control Room: *What?*
Harrison: *Okene Harrison.*
Control Room: *O...? What? Shit... I don't get that..*
Harrison: *Okene Harrison. Okay?*
Control Room: *Oklena Harrison?*
Harrison: *Okene, Okene!*
Control Room: *O'Connor?*

Harrison: [Spells out] *O-K-E-N-E.*

Nico: *He says 'Okene.'*

Harrison: *Yes, Okene.*

Control Room: [Spells] *O... K...*

Nico: *E-N-E*

Harrison: *O-K-E-N-E*

Control Room: *Okay, Okene, Okene Harrison.*

Harrison: *Yes, sir.*

Control Room: *Okay. Okay? You are a survivor Okene! Don't worry, we'll get you home, okay? Nice and easy!*

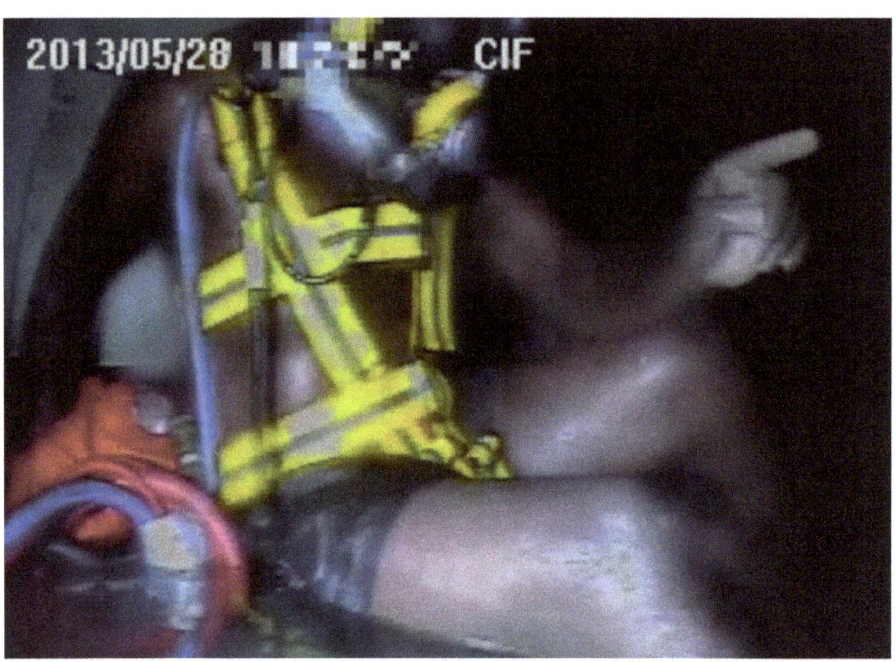

Authentic image of Harrison spelling out his name.

'When he said, "You're a survivor. We will get you out alive," I was simply so relieved and happy there. I was very, very happy. I had no idea how they were going to get me out, but I was just *so* happy,' Harrison remembers.

Harrison still didn't realize that what was about to happen to him was something no-one had ever attempted before. Of course, no-one was ever found underwater two and a half days after a ship had sunk. And particularly not deep inside a wreck at that depth.

I asked Tony how much time actually passed between when they found Harrison and when they were finally ready to get him out.

'From finding him, making a plan, getting everything organized, getting the diver's gear in there for him and then getting him ready to come out, it was in the neighbourhood of a little over three hours. Which is an awfully long time. He was extremely patient.'

In the control room, they crossed their fingers. At this stage, it was not a rescue operation … it was such an uncertain and unproven plan that the correct term for what they now embarked on was probably more a 'rescue attempt' than a proper operation.

Control Room: *Okay, let's get started. Can you hear me?*
Nico and Harrison: *Yes, Roger.*
Control Room: *How about you, Darryl, are you ready?*
Darryl: *Yeah… I'm ready.*
Control Room: *It's gonna be some work for you Darryl… you are in charge of two umbilicals now… three actually.. are you cool with that?*
Darryl: *Yes.*
Control Room: *You haven't tried that before, have you?*
Darryl: *No.*
Control Room: *It's going to be a lot more complicated than you think… tell them if they get stuck and you need help.*
Darryl: *Yeah, sure… eh.. help?… How?*
Control Room: *Yeah… uh…*

There is silence on the radio for a moment. Because Darryl is right. If something goes wrong now, there is no-one to help.

Control Room: *Hey, just make sure you handle it.*
Darryl: *Yes, Roger.*
Control Room: *[In the bell] André? We've dressed the survivor, he's wearing your helmet and harness now… and we're trying to get him out soon, okay?*
André: *I'm ready.*

All three divers were used to the fact that underwater tasks could be complicated. But in the past they had always had a protocol to follow. None of the people involved had ever been asked to do something they had not been trained to do or previously practiced. What they now had to do was completely new, and everyone — including the guys in dive control — knew it could go either way.

> **Control Room:** *Harrison?*
> **Harrison:** *Yes, sir?*
> **Control Room:** *What is your rank?*
> **Harrison:** *I'm the cook, I'm the cook.*
> **Control Room:** *Are you the cook?*
> **Harrison:** *Yes, sir.*
> **Control Room:** *... The cook always survives.*
>
> They all laugh.

In his quiet mind, Nico hoped that was true. To walk someone who's never been underwater before backwards, through an extremely complicated wreck, with not one, but two awkward, heavy air hoses trailing behind them, which could get stuck at any moment... and sporting an advanced diving helmet that most people would panic about wearing, even on land... it was not an easy task, and in a situation like that, the person can be as much a *cook who always survives* as you like. It was still going to be dangerous. Perhaps deadly.

> Up in the control room, they turn off Harrison's radio for a moment, so they can talk without him hearing them.
>
> **Control Room:** *Okay... does he panic when he gets underwater? Will he try to rip his helmet off or something? Or panic and attack you, Nico... Are you cool with that, Nico?*
> **Nico:** *Yep. I'm ready for it.*
> **Control Room:** *Alright, Nico and Darryl! Just be careful when you get him out... He'll grab onto everything and be panicky and erratic... He'll*

> probably grab you, Nico and maybe you too Daryl when he gets to you. And he will hold tight.
>
> **Nico:** *Yes, Roger.*
>
> **Control Room:** *He probably won't be able to rip your helmets off or anything. But it might be a bit of a struggle. You guys might have to use the harness to hold him... and pull him away from the wreckage and into the bell, okay? We'll take it as it comes.*

The divers are used to saying 'Yes' to what is asked of them by dive control—because usually the orders they get are part of a fixed routine, and not something they need to question. On the other hand, this is a task about as far from normal as you can possibly get, and there are a thousand questions they would like to ask. But both divers agree to try, because there are simply no other ideas on the table.

Harrison was even more in the dark: 'I had no idea what they were going to do or what I was going to do, I just knew I had to get out of the wreckage. I was very happy. I had a wonderful feeling in me... and I had understood that they were planning to save me... to get me out of the wreckage.'

But what to do if he panicked?

Tony explains the harsh reality: 'Well, if he panicked... if he had fought back or gone for the diver, then we had to... make a really hard decision... then Nico would have to leave him. That was the rule.'

Tony sits for a bit, as if digesting his own words. Then he nods.

In the control room, they turn Harrison's radio back on.

> **Control Room:** *Okay, are we ready? Harrison?*
> **Harrison:** *Yes.*
> **Control Room:** *Okay. You have to go with Nico—out, okay?*
> **Harrison:** *Yes, sir.*
> **Control Room:** *Out of Jascon 4, okay?*
> **Harrison:** *Yes, sir.*

But what was Nico thinking when he got the signal to start?

'For me, the scariest thing was just getting his head under the water. It's different when you wear a regular diving mask with a snorkel on it — you can't compare it. If you have a helmet, like ours, and you put your head in the water for the first time, it's not an easy one. Really not. It's not even nice the first time when you're *not* underwater. If you are even the slightest bit claustrophobic, it will scare the shit out of you. I've never seen anyone who doesn't panic. Even people who are used to diving.'

> It may sound relatively harmless to be close to a person who is panicking, but you have to remember where this is taking place. Nico is pressed right up against Harrison, inside a cramped room almost completely full of water. There are many things on Nico's equipment that can be pulled, turned, or torn to pieces. His helmet in particular is exposed, because the equipment is just not designed for this kind of situation. If Nico's helmet gets damaged or mishandled, neither of them will get out of there alive.

Tony was cautious, 'So … we must never put anyone's life in danger … But there is always doubt about the outcome when you take a chance like this. So, Nico just had to be ready for Harrison to attack him.'

Darryl, who was outside the wreck, couldn't come in to help and André in the bell couldn't dive because Harrison was wearing his helmet. So, the plan was simply that nothing *could* go wrong. There was no back-up plan.

> Inside the small cramped cabin that had been Harrison's prison for almost three days, Nico slowly helped him into the water. Now it would start to get dangerous.
>
> **Control Room:** *Okay. Let's get started. You keep your air hose, Harrison. Hold it with both hands at all times and never move your hands. Nico will also hold on to you. You must not hold on to him. Just keep both hands on your hose. Continually.*

In fact, there was no technical reason for asking Harrison to hold on to the air hose with both hands. But they knew it would make it more difficult for him to grab Nico if he suddenly panicked. Wearing the diving helmet, Nico had fairly limited vision. Positioning Harrison's hands directly in front of him, holding the hose, meant that they were constantly in Nico's line of sight as he walked backwards holding on to Harrison's harness. And Nico would hopefully have time to react if Harrison let go of the air hose.

Control Room: *And you listen to me, okay? We're trying now. Put your head under the water and breathe, okay?*

Nico held on to him, 'So he could feel that everything was under control and that he didn't have to hold on to me. That would make it easier to control him when he panicked. Because we all knew that he would. When I took him into the water, I was fully convinced that he would try to rip the helmet off, pull himself back up, or freak out.'

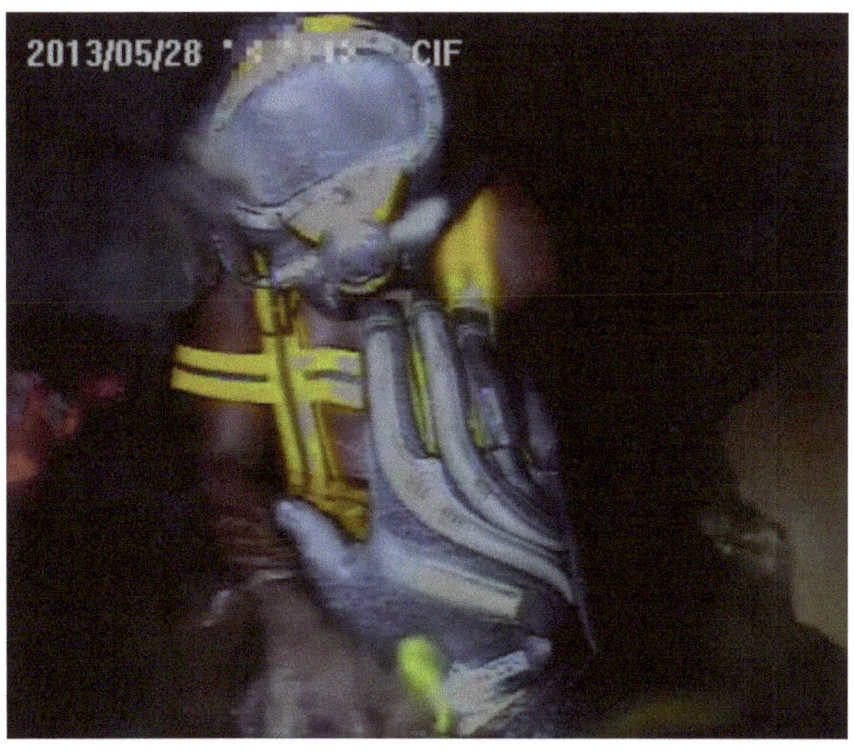

Authentic photo of Nico holding Harrison back just before they try to dive out of the wreckage.

> Nico carefully pulls Harrison down towards the surface, where the pitch-black water begins. Harrison has to keep his head underwater, so they can move into the narrow wreck.
>
> **Nico:** *Just relax, Harrison.*
>
> Nico gently pulls on Harrison's hands, so that he has the best possible control over him in the water and, if panic occurs, he can restrain him.
> Harrison dips his head underwater and disappears into bubbles in the dark.
>
> **Control Room:** *Okay, how's it going? Are you okay, Harrison?*
>
> There is silence for a moment.
>
> **Harrison:** *Yes, that's fine, sir.*

Nico was surprised, 'He was totally cool. And I was delighted at how calm he was. Impressive.'

> Harrison calmly begins to move after Nico. Nico is completely concentrated on the task of guiding Harrison down the narrow stairwell as best he can. But deep down, he's totally amazed at how cool Harrison is.

Harrison explains his mindset, 'I've never tried diving before. But I know that in such a situation, it is obvious that I should panic. But if I panic, I'm going to die. So, when I find myself in such a situation, the only thing on my mind is "calm yourself first and figure out a way to get through it."'

> Harrison calmly follows Nico. Nico keeps a firm grip on Harrison's harness with one hand and holds Harrison's hands tightly around his air hose with the other, so that Harrison walks with his hands on the hose in front of him, between them, the whole time.
>
> **Control Room:** *Just keep a tight grip on your air hose Harrison.*

Harrison: *Roger.*
Control Room: *Don't let go okay? We'll get you home.*

Harrison, of course, is not used to the heavy diving helmet, and no-one in the dive team has thought about how long it took them to get used to one back when they were learning. It's something very unfamiliar the first time anyone tries it, and extremely uncomfortable. The dive team may not have thought of it, but at this point it dawns on Harrison. His helmet dangles from side to side and, exhausted from the long stay in the flooded cabin, he has no strength to control it. He knocks the helmet into the sides of the wreck and into Nico's face. Nico has to make a big effort just to keep Harrison's body free of himself and things they are passing.

Nico does not dare to let go of Harrison's hands, because it is important that he is guided very precisely through the narrow corridors and that Nico can hold him if he panics. Harrison's heavy helmet knocks into the glass of Nico's helmet again and again.

'The problem is that I didn't have the strength to control the hat myself. I struggled with it because I didn't imagine it would be so heavy,' Harrison recalls.

Nico had plenty to do. He realized that even though Harrison was calm, they still had a long way to go, and a lot could go wrong. The worst thing he could do now would be to relax and start thinking everything would go fine.

Control Room: *Harrison, hold your air hose... Don't let go, okay? And just breathe easy, Harrison, you're doing very, very well.*

And crawling out through the wreck is no cakewalk. Nico has to creep backwards so that he can face Harrison, maintaining eye contact with him at all times. He has to keep Harrison close, so that he can steer him safely through passages so narrow that Nico had previously had difficulty with them on his own, and walking forwards.

Nico can see why it was so difficult: 'It was some struggle with the two umbilicals, because Darryl was so far away and outside the wreckage. He heaved and struggled to steer and pull both of them to prevent the umbilicals — and thereby us — from getting stuck on the way out.'

The long umbilicals wound through the interior of the complicated wreck, around corners and through doorways and up and down stairs. Slowly, they had to be pulled outwards — at the same pace as Nico and Harrison moved. Nico had to constantly inform Darryl as to whether he needed to pull faster or slower to avoid the hoses piling up inside the wreck or getting too taught. In either case, they may have become stuck on one of the many obstacles in the wreck.

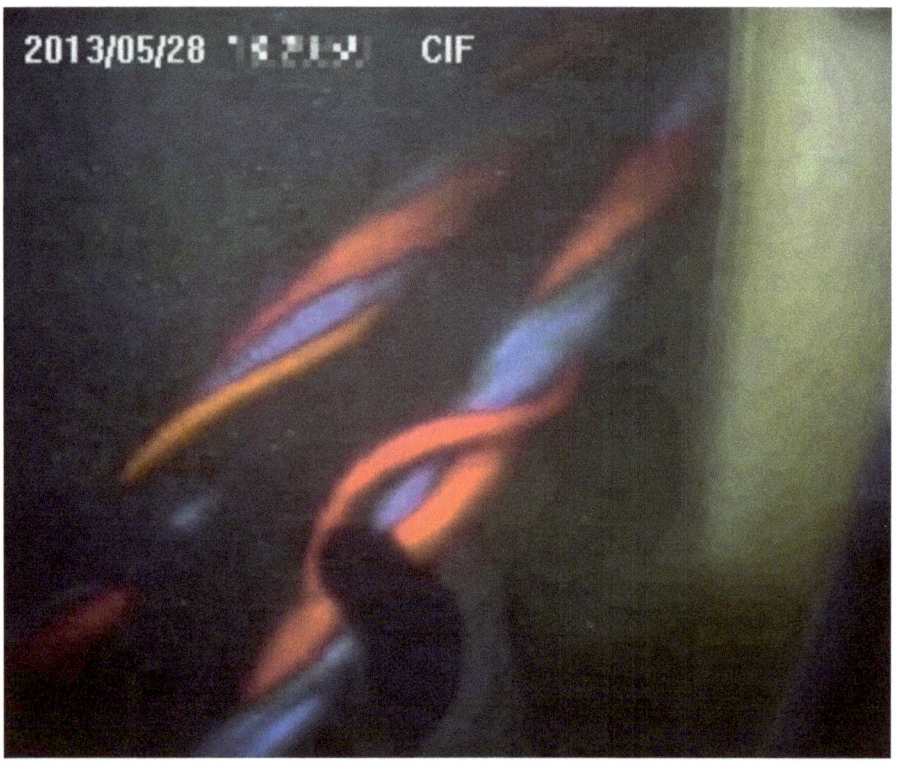

Authentic footage of Darryl's point of view — outside the wreck — trying to keep track of both Harrison and Nico's long, heavy diving hoses.

Nico: *Darryl? Keep pulling! Keep pulling both umbilicals!*
Darryl: *Received.*

Darryl continues to pull both umbilicals outward.

Nico: *Keep pulling out Darryl! More on mine.*
Control Room: *Keep pulling out Darryl. Okay, talk to each other guys.*
Nico: *Pull... now on both.*
Darryl: *Roger. Trying...*

This must have been extremely difficult for Nico, but Darryl's task was not easy, either. If he had made a mistake or pulled too much or too little on the two different heavy umbilicals it could easily have ruined everything.

Nico was not enjoying it: 'Now I was squeezing backwards through a room that was cramped for one person going forewords, now we were two people ... and I was trying to get him through the passage backwards without being able to see what was behind me.'

Control Room: *Just hold on to your air hose, Harrison... what we're doing is we're taking you up the stairs and you're going up to the next floor... which is below you, okay? So, you guys have to see if you can get down the narrow stairs, okay?*

Contrary to what everyone had predicted, Harrison behaved in a completely exemplary manner during the complicated trip out through the wreck. A hint of optimism began to spread through the control room. But at that point they hadn't yet realized that they had overlooked a very important detail, which would shortly have major consequences.

So far, Harrison was doing exactly what they asked him to do, and at no point was he even close to panicking. That surprised Tony.

'A lot. I mean, this is someone who has never been underwater. I think at that time he must have been quite anxious about being underwater, after what he had experienced, and he must have been completely exhausted and probably quite traumatized because he had been underwater for so long. I mean ... he thought he was going to die down there. But the way he'd been behaving ... it was true proof that he just *wanted* to live.'

Harrison's own view was, 'All I thought about was getting off the ship and now I would get to see my family ... And I just imagined that — soon I was out of the wreck and safe on a ship.'

Harrison likely had no idea where they were on the inverted wreck, as he was busy trying to keep his helmet from banging into Nico and the walls. Still, dive control maintained close contact with him the whole time to divert his thoughts and reassure him that the path to safety was getting shorter all the time. Unfortunately, that meant that the 'detail' they had overlooked ceased to be a detail and became, in Harrison's mind, something very concrete.

> **Control Room:** *Okay Harrison, what we do is, once you've come through the stairs, you come to where the captain's cabin is, okay? Harrison?*
> **Harrison:** *Yes.*
> **Control Room:** *Yeah, you have to say 'Roger,' okay? So I know you're okay.*
> **Harrison:** *Roger.*
> **Control Room:** *All right. You are doing very well.*

Despite that assertion, Harrison couldn't assess their progress: 'I knew the way out, because it was a ship I'd worked on for years, so the whole structure of it was in my head, but on the way out through the wreck, at no point did I know where I was — because my diving hat was placed in the way, so I could see virtually nothing. I didn't have a light in my helmet. Nico's hat had a lamp, but it shone right into my face, so I couldn't see anything. I only saw something when Nico occasionally turned his head while pulling me, but I couldn't see properly.'

Even though he *could* see a little, Nico did not find it easy: 'It was very difficult, and I had to really concentrate because it was dangerous. The visibility was very poor and was not improved by the fact that there were now two of us messing it up, so I don't want to say that it would have helped much to go forward with him, the dangerous thing was being two, where the one had never been underwater before. Just being inside such a wreck is dangerous… even if you're experienced. And going backwards doesn't make it any safer because I had to think what's next in every step and there was always a risk of something getting stuck when you go backwards. When you move backwards, you cannot feel when you are stuck in the same way as if you go forwards. It's not a very smart way to move.'

Tony explains the mood in dive control: 'There wasn't really anything we could do — other than keep close radio contact with all of them. Of course, it's not easy because … I mean … Nico tried to pull him out, simultaneously controlling his umbilical *and* the other umbilical. And the backup diver, Darryl, was far away — outside the wreck. Darryl tugged and tugged at both umbilicals to get them both out alive. It was extremely dangerous.'

Harrison though, wasn't afraid: 'Because I had complete trust in them … they said, "You have to go with Nico and Nico will help you out." Nico took my hands and walked in front … even though he was walking backwards, I believed he knew the way so he could get me out. I couldn't see anything, but I trusted that he knew what he was doing and just followed him and did what they said.'

Everyone knew that while it was dangerous getting Harrison out through the wreck, it would become still more critical as they got close to the exit and Harrison realized they were out. How would he react?

Only at that point did it begin to dawn on them that perhaps there was something they had overlooked. They hadn't thought to prepare Harrison for what was going to happen when they got out of the wreck, or made a plan for what to do themselves. Everything had been about getting Harrison out. But from that point there was still a long and complicated road before he was safely on land.

> **Control Room:** [Without Harrison hearing] *We'll just have to think that this guy, he's never been underwater before… this ocean, it's going to look very big and overwhelming to him, when he comes out of the wreckage… so if anything happens, if he panics, just hold on tight to him and drag him to the diving bell as fast as you can and shove his head in there, okay?*
> **Nico:** *Roger, got it.*
> **Control Room:** [Still without Harrison hearing] *Of course, he has no idea what the hell is going to happen now.*

Nico and Harrison were almost out of the wreck. They came down the long hallway that led to the door which Nico and Darryl had first broken open, where Darryl stood waiting for them, pulling on their air hoses. Darryl saw the flickering light from Nico's lamp some distance inside the wreck, and Harrison — as they rounded the last corner — could see the exit to the ship's outer deck for the first time in three days. At the end of the corridor was a doorway into the dark, but blue, Atlantic Ocean.

Nico remembers thinking about how Harrison might react: 'I was very aware of how Harrison took it and that he didn't panic. It didn't matter what the instructions were and what was planned for us to do. I was responsible for him, and when we did this, I had an overwhelming sense of responsibility. If I made a mistake, it could cost him his life. It really weighed heavy inside me.'

> Nico and Harrison carefully walk the last short distance to the exit.
>
> **Control Room:** *Okay, Harrison, we're almost there and you're doing a very good job. Now Nico slowly helps you up past the chief engineer's cabin and we get to the door — and the outside of the vessel, okay?*

'You can't really see anything inside the wreckage so I had no idea where I was... but when I suddenly saw the sight of the deep blue water outside the door... it was so blue... so blue... then I knew: I'm out of the boat. Saved!' Harrison recalls.

> Everyone is tense and holding their breath. This is when things could go wrong. If they start to relax — let their guard down — then this could get dangerous. But an inner joy fills them all, at having made it this far.
> Still keeping a firm grip on him, Nico pulls Harrison the last bit of the way to the door and stands waiting in the threshold.
>
> **Nico:** *We're outside now.*
> **Control Room:** *Okay, you guys are out...*

Darryl, who has really been struggling with the two heavy umbilicals, barely has time to get a quick 'thumbs up' from Nico, before he's sent ahead to the diving bell. There, he will pull their umbilicals up, so that they can get Harrison into the diving bell.

Nico is alone with Harrison on the wreck again. What could really go wrong now...? Well, a lot.

Control Room: *Okay Harrison, just stay there. Now I'm just going to send the one diver — Darryl — over to the diving bell so he can help you get over there. Nico is with you.*

It was at that point that the detail they had all overlooked during the planning phase of the rescue operation, was to be revealed. A detail with potentially disastrous consequences.

Tony confesses: 'One of the things we didn't really think about when we were planning the rescue was, that Harrison had no idea what a diving bell was. So, when we got to the outside of the wreck and we told him to go over to the diving bell, he didn't understand what was being said to him at all.'

Control Room: *Hello, my friend, can you hear me?*
Harrison: *Yes, I can.*
Control Room: *Okay, now don't panic, okay? You have to listen to me, okay? We take you inside the diving bell. Okay?*

In the urgency to get him out of the wreck safely, no-one had thought to inform Harrison what the next part of the plan entailed, and why it was important. No-one had considered whether Harrison understood what a diving bell was or what it was used was for.

'I had no idea I was going to a bell, because I had never seen a diving bell before in my life.'

For sat divers, the diving bell is the *only* way up and down from a dive. But of course, not for ordinary divers. When they finish a dive, they swim upwards towards the surface.

'The divers I've seen, they just jump in from a boat, so I was sure I'd be taken up to a boat on the surface of the water. So naturally that's what I prepared for. I had no idea how deep we were.'

The divers' plan, however, was to get Harrison to safety inside the pressurized diving bell, then pull it up onto the ship and put him in a pressure chamber, where he could slowly decompress to avoid dying of decompression sickness (the bends). But Harrison thought that the only way you could be saved from a sunken ship was by getting on board a boat. And, of course, boats are at sea level.

Nico recalls the point when he finally had Harrison outside the wreck: 'There was a diving bell in front of him, something he'd never seen in his life before. It looked like a spaceship with all the lights. Not a place you'd want to swim to if you didn't know what it was.'

> Harrison stands looking around in confusion. He has no idea what is happening.
>
> **Control Room:** *Harrison?*
> **Harrison:** *Yes?*
>
> The divers have run a green rope between the wreck and the diving bell so they can pull themselves back and forth between the two. This is what Harrison is now supposed to do, with Nico, to get safely inside the bell.
>
> **Control Room:** *Okay, see the green rope that leads you to the bell?*
>   *Nico? Show him the green rope, so he can hold the green rope.*
>
> Nico takes Harrison's hand and gently places it on the green rope.
>
> **Nico:** *Okay... look! Grab the green rope...*
> **Control Room:** *We'll take you into the bell. Okay? Hold the green rope.*
>
> Harrison is confused. He doesn't grab the green rope even though Nico tries to take his hand and put it on the rope. It's important to get Harrison into the diving bell because that's the only way they can get him up. But Harrison still doesn't grab the rope.

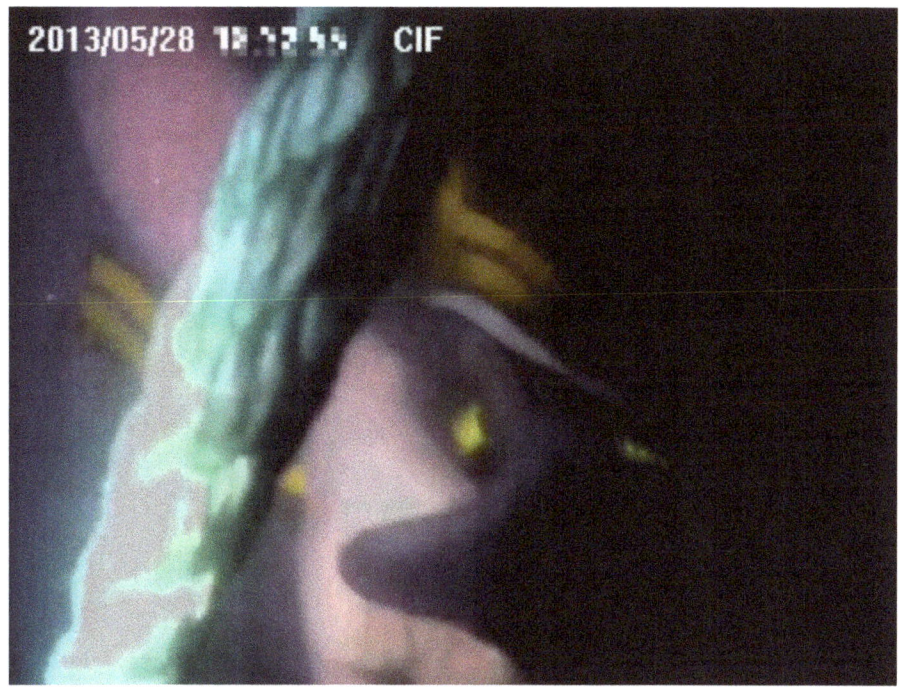
Authentic footage of Harrison trying to grab the green rope.

What was the problem?

Nico watched it unfold: 'He touched the rope. And then I saw... he was just floating in the water.'

Harrison thought he could grab the rope but, 'Before I could... I kind of floated away from it. I didn't have the strength to hold on to the green rope. I felt myself floating and the whole thing spinning. I thought that if I took a few swims — I would come to the surface. That was what I thought was the plan... that they would take me to the surface. So, I swam up. Or tried to.'

Harrison let himself float upwards because that is where he believed rescue was. But upwards was certain death.

Tony spells out how dangerous this was: 'Because Harrison had been down to a depth of thirty-four metres for sixty-eight hours at that point, it was important that he didn't go to the surface quickly. If he tried to do so, bubbles would be released into his bloodstream. And as I said, it can cause cardiac arrest, brain damage and... yes... death.'

Harrison was soon in trouble: 'I didn't understand the green rope thing and started swimming to the surface because I thought we were going to board a rescue ship. But I fainted as soon as I got a little way up. I heard Nico say, "He's passed out, he's passed out," but I couldn't move ... I just floated up.'

> Harrison's hand releases the green rope and he begins to swim upwards. Then he stops moving but is still speeding up towards the surface of the sea far above them. Nico tries to hold on to Harrison's foot but loses his grip. He frantically calls dive control, who can see what he sees.
>
> **Nico:** *He's floating away from me ... upward ... I'm losing him! He's passed out!*
> **Control Room:** *What?*
> **Nico:** *He's passed out!*
> **Control Room:** *Oh, did he pass out?*
> **Nico:** *Yeah, I'm trying to pull him down by the umbilical.*
>
> Nico tries to stop Harrison's buoyancy by pulling on his umbilical, but there are floating umbilicals all over the water and Harrison's is so long that pulling on it doesn't help ... They all know that rising up quickly will kill Harrison.

Harrison continued up towards the surface with no-one able to stop him. Divers like Nico wear rubber boots — not flippers — and a heavy lead vest to stay on the bottom. They can't swim at all, even if they try. They are much too heavy. So, Nico couldn't get hold of Harrison, who disappeared upwards above him.

> **Control Room:** *Catch him! Stop him!*
> **Nico:** *He floats up.*

Harrison hadn't been given a lead vest to wear. It was not deemed necessary for the journey out through the wreck and the short distance across to the diving bell. He was only wearing a diving helmet, which was filled with air and therefore buoyant. Like a beach ball held underwater, it rose towards the surface, and the higher it got, the more powerful the buoyancy inside became. So, the helmet would continue to rise upwards with greater and greater speed if it was not stopped and held down.

Control Room: *Get him in the bell, drag him, drag him!*
Nico: *I see him, I see him.*

Dive control thinks — wrongly — that he is not getting any oxygen in his helmet and tells André in the bell, to send more oxygen and helium to it. But that doesn't change anything. Harrison is passed out because he is rising towards the surface — towards certain death.

Control Room: *Open his gas from inside the bell, open all the gas!*

Nico quickly loses any chance to stop the unconscious and rapidly rising Harrison, and for the first time during the extremely complicated three-hour long rescue operation, everyone panics.

Control Room: *Open his freeflow! Pull him down with the air hose, pull him down!*

Nico felt his efforts were futile: 'I followed Harrison by pulling on his umbilical, but there was so much umbilical floating out in the water, because we only had one person to take care of all of our umbilicals when we got out of the wreck, that there was maybe twenty metres of extra umbilical that was now just floating around in the water... so I was getting nowhere pulling on his umbilical... I couldn't keep up with him. I just saw his feet in front of me as he rose to the surface.'

Control Room: *Open his gas! Pull him, pull him!*

Fortunately, the other diver, Darryl, had made it to the diving bell just before Harrison passed out. He quickly climbed to the very top of the bell. From there he could plunge into the nothingness of the vast Atlantic Ocean and make a grab for Harrison.

Darryl: *I got him!*

Darryl takes Harrison down under the bell. Nico arrives and together they move him towards the hatch at the bottom of the bell. The disaster has been averted.

Control Room: *Okay, pop his head in. Pull him! Get your head in the bell.*
Nico: *Roger. We have him here. Good job Darryl.*
Control Room: *Open... so he can crawl inside. Help him.*
Nico: *He's in the bell.*

12

Three Went Down, Four Came Up

Confused, Harrison came to inside the bell. André quickly pulled off Harrison's diving helmet, and he looked around in astonishment at the tiny bell.

'When they took my hat off, they called out if I was okay... and I said, "I'm okay, I'm okay."'

Control Room: *How are you, Harrison?*
Harrison: *I'm fine, sir.*
Control Room: *Okay... well, you scared me there.*
Harrison: *Sorry.*

Via a camera in the bell, the control room can see Harrison looking around in confusion.

Control Room: *Are you okay in the bell, Harrison?*
Harrison: *I'm fine, sir.*
Control Room: *Just give me a thumbs up!*

André shows Harrison the camera up in the ceiling of the bell and Harrison gives the camera a thumbs up.

Control Room: *Good job my friend, well done! You are a survivor!*

'I had no idea where I was. I didn't know I was still underwater. In fact, I never knew I was inside a diving bell, because I had never seen a diving bell before. I don't know what it looks like. I don't even think I've seen a movie with them in it... I just know when I got into the diving bell, I asked myself,

"Where the hell am I? How am I going to get out of this place?" I was just waiting to see what would happen next…'

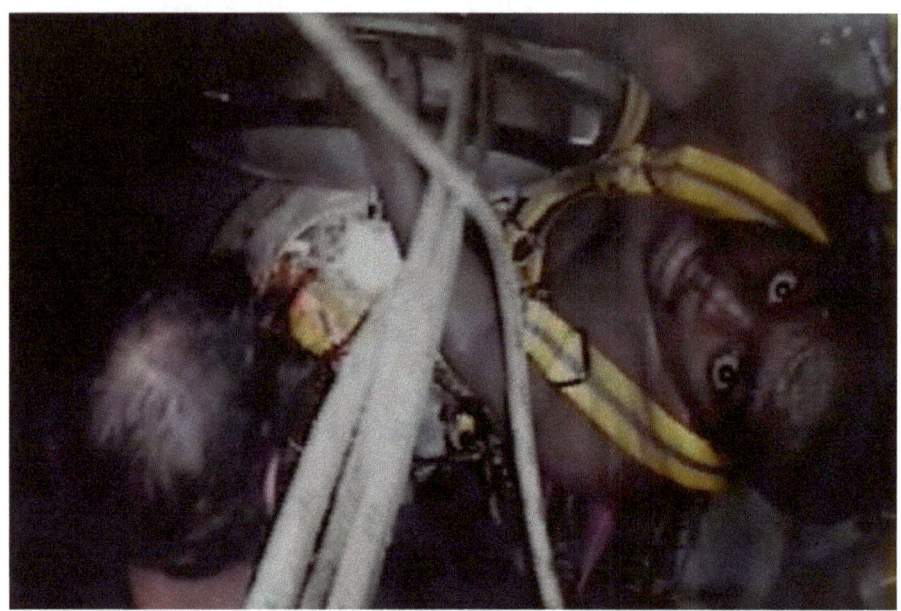

Authentic footage of a disoriented Harrison giving a thumbs up just as he regained consciousness inside the diving bell.

In the water below the diving bell, Nico and Darryl are giving each other high fives. They are relieved, happy and — especially with their squeaky Mickey Mouse voices — seem like two over-excited schoolboys who a moment ago scored a crucial goal. But what they have just achieved is unimaginable. It is unprecedented — a hugely impressive rescue operation, like no other.

Control Room: *Damn, I'm impressed. Okay guys. You all did a great job, thank you. Nico. Darryl, André, well done. Really, you guys have made me proud.*

Once Nico and Darryl have packed up the long, uncontrolled umbilicals they also crawl into the diving bell … or at least they try to.

Nico couldn't see how they could all fit inside: 'Harrison had entered the bell and was safe so far. But such a diving bell is designed for three people, not four people. Before, it was difficult to be in there, the three of us, because both me and Darryl are quite big ... but now it was almost impossible to squeeze in. I remember that I, as the last one to crawl in, looked up from the hole at the bottom and thought, "This is not going to work ... There is no room for all four of us."'

Both Nico and Darryl managed to get into the little bell, but Nico was right, there was actually not enough room for them.

'We had to stuff Harrison up against the top of the bell, just to get enough room for us to close the hatch. But it worked out in the end, even though it was pretty tight.'

Exhausted but safe, Harrison was baffled by his new surroundings: 'I was like, "Where the hell am I?" I had no idea why we were there. Or why they had gotten me in there. I don't really remember the last time underwater and suddenly I was in this very, very cramped little metal room, full of buttons and equipment and a man I hadn't seen before. But they took my helmet off and I could breathe, so I thought I was probably not underwater anymore but inside a boat. After Nico came in and the other guy came in and took their helmets off, I could see their faces but there was hardly any room for us. There was no room for us at all, but then a radio voice said, "Okay, we are getting ready to hoist you up" and then I thought I would see what was going to happen next.'

> **Control Room:** *Alright guys, are you ready to come up?*
> **André:** *Roger.*
> **Control Room:** *We went down with three, came back with four!* [They all laugh]. *Well done boys! Damn Nico! Nice work boys ... Darryl, well done. André, well done. It was fantastic, man ...*

They all climb up the sides of the round bell and hold on to the equipment there in order to close the hatch at the bottom. All the way up to the vessel, they have to stand in a close embrace due to lack of space and Harrison even lies right up against the top.

As they realised their success, Nico felt conflicted: 'We wanted to celebrate that we'd found Harrison, and of course we were all very happy, but it was strange to be happy when we had been ... at the same time busy putting dead sailors in body bags. There were probably still several bodies inside the wreckage, which we had to go in and collect afterwards.'

Harrison too wasn't sure how to feel: 'Inside the bell I was told that I was the only survivor from the accident, and it was a strange feeling to be happy to be alive and at the same time unhappy that so many friends' lives had been lost.'

'The whole experience on the wreck made me think that life is so fragile, and it can be taken away in an instant.' Nico reflected.

Then the bell was brought back to the diving ship. Harrison was back, if not on land, then back to safety.

Harrison still didn't understand what was going on: 'After some time, the door opened, and they said: "We have to go through here." I was like ... What? Where are we? I did not know that we were now up on the big vessel on the surface. I thought we were still underwater somehow.'

When a diving bell comes up onto a diving vessel, it is automatically connected to a pressure chamber, where the divers have to decompress to avoid diving sickness. They sit there for a while — still under controlled pressure — after which they can move into another chamber, where they live for the twenty-eight days they are on the job as sat divers. Harrison was taken into the pressure chamber so that, very slowly over thirty-six hours, they could get him back to the pressure on the surface, so he would not suffer serious injuries after his long stay underwater.

Harrison again: 'I didn't understand anything. They said, "Come this way" — and I tried to get out of the bell, but they had to support me, because my legs were completely exhausted from standing up so long in the cold water ... We entered a metal room, and I could see that we were somewhere else again, but still inside these strange metal surroundings. Later I found out that it was the decompression chamber, and I was now properly on board the large diving vessel. But at that time, I didn't know where I was. I didn't know I wasn't still underwater somehow. I just felt like I was okay, so that's fine and it was great to be out of the wreckage. But they didn't tell me anything. They probably thought I knew what had happened. They kept saying, "We're going to check your pulse, we're going to check that, you're going to do this, you're going to do that." So, I was like, "Okay, whatever" ... I was so tired and let them do whatever they wanted.'

Harrison was regularly examined throughout his decompression because it is far from healthy to have a three-day stay at a depth of thirty-four metres. In fact no-one could believe that he'd come through it without injury.

'They had a phone in the decompression chamber, and they asked me if I wanted to call my wife to tell her I wasn't dead. She didn't know I was alive. For three days she had thought I was dead, like the others on board. But when I called her, she hung up.'

Harrison didn't consider that his voice had changed. On the wreck and in the pressure tank, he had inhaled helium and oxygen, and the helium had given him that shrill Mickey Mouse voice.

'She didn't think it was me because I sounded so weird ... she thought someone was playing a sick joke on her ... So, I had to borrow an iPad from one of the divers inside the chamber and we took a picture of me in there and sent it to her Facebook, so she could see it was me and I was still alive. And then she fainted. After all, she had been told that I went down with the vessel and was dead. For three days she had believed it. So ... she was so shocked that she passed out when she saw me alive in the picture. So, her mother, who was with her, had to rush to get her back on her feet. And then she just cried. She was very relieved to hear that I was alive. When she finally believed it.'

Nico and Harrison didn't get to talk after they got on the ship: 'Unfortunately. The last time I saw Harrison after we rescued him was when he went into the decompression chamber. He was only a short time in the chamber with me, where I gave him some clothes, as he was only wearing a pair of boxer shorts. I would have liked to spend some time with him and talk a little, but he had to go into another pressure chamber because I had to prepare for further dives.'

Harrison felt the same: 'It was a shame. I wanted to talk to Nico. There was so much I wanted to ask him and share with him, and I felt like we had become friends even though we had never really spoken for real ... but I was only in the pressure chamber with Nico for ten to fifteen minutes, because then I had to be decompressed in another chamber and he was sent back. He gave me some clothes and we just took a picture; got a chocolate and the next moment I went into another decompression chamber. Then I didn't see Nico anymore... he was back underwater again and they took me to a helicopter. We took some pictures with some of the crew, including Tony, who I didn't get to talk to either for real, and I got into a helicopter so I could get to the hospital and after that went home to my family.'

Nico again, 'You get close to another person in such a situation, and I felt that what we had been through together had made us some kind of friends. But even though I really wanted to spend some time with Harrison, it was a good ending to the story for me, knowing now that he was safe, he was fine, he was on his way home, and he could see his family again.'

Once Harrison was safe, the divers were sent back to the wreck. There was no time to celebrate because the task was far from over.

'As soon as we found someone alive, we went from body recovery mode to rescue mode immediately.'

From the time Nico climbed out of the diving bell to begin the search for bodies and knocked open the door to the wreck, till the time they were back with Harrison in the bell, Nico's dive had lasted eleven hours. It was — even for sat divers — a grotesquely long dive. Now the entire ship's concentration turned again to getting divers back into search mode, including Nico.

Tony explains: 'We got divers in the water as fast as we could... There could be more alive down there in other air pockets, we hoped there was a chance.'

Although it was a joyful moment and many people wanted to celebrate the fact that Harrison had been found alive, it would have been hard for Harrison to join in while also mourning the loss of eleven friends, who had not been so lucky. But now there was a sudden commotion on the big dive ship. Could more of Harrison's buddies still be alive down there?

Several divers searched the wreck, and all areas of the large, overturned ship were thoroughly checked for survivors.

Tony: 'We were hoping to find more survivors. But unfortunately, that was not the case. We found the rest of the crew... except for one, we couldn't find him. He was not on board. But we found eleven out of twelve people who had been on board.'

Authentic photo of the three divers, Nico, André and Darryl, together with Harrison in the pressure tank.

Harrison had to accept that he was the only member of the crew who had made it. Although others had survived for a while in smaller air pockets elsewhere on the ship, he was the only one still alive after the sixty-two hours it took to be found. After a short hospital check-up in Nigeria, he was able to drive home to his family.

'When I got back to my home later, my wife ran out … she hugged me, and she was rolling on the ground. Then she said that she didn't cry, even though it really looked like … she said that what she did was that she thanked God for protecting me, for keeping me alive so we could be together again. She was just so happy. And so was I. It was a good day, and all the neighbours came and wanted to touch me because they simply couldn't believe it had happened.'

Harrison with his then wife after coming ashore.

13

On Land Again... and Into the Water... Again

Finally back on dry land, Harrison received fairly rudimentary medical care: 'I got checked out at a clinic right when I got ashore, and they asked me to come in every day for the next few days. I did that for three days, until the doctor said that now I was okay and could just go home. But I knew I was definitely not okay. Because water was constantly coming out of one ear. Something must have happened to the eardrum when I fainted and ascended too quickly, or I could not stand the long stay at the great depth of the sea. Anyway, I had big problems with my ear.

'I called my employer, who was responsible for the accident, and they asked me to go to their own medical clinic, because it didn't cost them that much to treat me there. I went there and they couldn't really help. The ear was completely destroyed. I spoke to my employer again, but they now said that their doctor had said that everything was fine and I could easily return to work.

'I told them I was not okay at all. I couldn't even hear what they were saying properly. Water came out of my ear and there was tremendous pain inside my head. But they said they couldn't help anymore because their doctor said I was fine. They obviously weren't interested in spending more money on me, but I wasn't okay. In many ways. Also because water had become a trauma for me. When I closed my eyes, I was back inside the wreck and every time I tried to sleep... I had nightmares about being trapped underwater again. I couldn't be near water... not even a beach or a swimming pool.

'On the way home from the doctor's clinic, I drove with a friend who had a car. I was driving and he was sleeping in the passenger seat, but on the way over a bridge there was a roundabout where a lady pulled out directly in front of me. I could see that she had two children in the back seat, but there was no way around hitting her. Or there was one... and that was to turn the car off the road, so I did that. We drove straight through a palm tree and the car fell over the bridge and straight into the water. All I saw was darkness. The water hammered into the cabin, and I could feel that we were upside down and headed for the seabed. When we landed on the seabed, I could feel that I was trapped under the water. Again.

'I couldn't get out because my door and side window were sunk into the mud. I unbuckled my seat belt and opened the opposite door. I was back under the sea. That was a bad situation. But this time I managed to get to the surface and get some air. There I discovered that my friend had not gotten out of the car. He had been asleep when we drove into the water and must still be trapped inside the car on the seabed. So, there was no way around it. I had to dive back down. I found him inside the car, where he was unconscious. I got his door open and got his seat belt off and lifted him out and up to the surface. He was completely confused. He had no idea what had happened. I told him we had had an accident.

'During the accident, my employer's crew bus came by. The bus that takes the crew to and from the ships. The bus had stopped and they discovered that it was me who had been in the accident and had been trapped inside the car underwater. The bus driver, who knew me well, glared at me and said, 'You … again?? Who is trying to kill you?"

'Then I borrowed a motorbike so I could get home.'

What are the odds of the same person being caught underwater twice in a row? What goes through one's mind in such a situation, when — once again — one is trapped underwater, locked in a metal box. Don't you feel yourself transported straight back into the nightmare, on the Atlantic seabed?

'All that was going on was, "How do I get out?" When I had smashed my side window and could feel that side was buried in mud, I went for the other side of the car and got that door open. And out. I wasn't going to be trapped underwater again. But it was actually mostly when I got to the surface and saw the bus with all my colleagues standing and staring at me. They thought it was God's intervention that had saved me … that I was the kind of person who just can't die. That was probably where I was most affected by it. So, I rushed to borrow a motorbike so I could get away from it all.'

But it's not normal to survive two episodes like that in such a short time.

'Nah … It's not normal. Maybe God has some plan for me. It's like those who want to kill me aren't really successful at it. But it convinced me that I should probably be careful with what I do. So that I always remember. You are responsible for your own safety. No-one else looks after that shop. I live each day as if it were the last.'

Harrison had no great desire to return to being a ship's cook. He was not offered any psychological treatment or any form of compensation for the tragic and traumatic experience he had been through, so he just stayed at home. He tried to get compensation, but since the official explanation for the sinking of the ship was that it was the captain's mistake — because he had been sailing in rough weather with an open cargo hatch into which water had entered — the families of the drowned sailors only got a small symbolic compensation payment. Since Harrison had survived the accident, he received no compensation at all.

Harrison found it hard to believe that the captain had sailed with an open hatch. He wouldn't have made a mistake like that — and what he experienced when the ship sank was not at all the feeling of a ship slowly taking in too much water. It would have taken a very long time for a ship that size to fill with water through a single small hatch. It was more the sensation of something instantly turning the whole ship upside down. But the case seemed clear and there was nothing more to discuss.

'My employer kept pushing me to come back to work. But I couldn't go out to sea again. Water had become a trauma for me. The panic, the anxiety, the dark, the animals that ate me... it had become a phobia... I was so afraid of water. Even in my own house, when I sleep in my bed, I feel that the bed is sinking, that the whole house is sinking. So, when I wake up to run out, my wife grabs me and says, "Calm down, you're inside a house, this isn't a boat, just calm down."'

Harrison was traumatised and there was no way he would be able to work on a ship again — or for that matter even stay close to the sea. But since he had received no compensation after the accident, he had to find a way to support his family.

'I didn't get any real compensation from the accident. But the same company that owned the sunken vessel asked me to come back and work with them, this time in a very small office.'

Harrison had no other way to earn a living and it is not easy having no income in Nigeria. So he accepted the job, even though it was a very long way from his home. And the job was anything but appealing.

'I wasn't going near water. I simply wouldn't be able to do that. So, my employer put me in a small office, far as hell from my family, so I could only get home on the weekends. The salary they gave me was so low and I had to pay for a place to live nearby myself. It was a really bad job.'

Harrison was not the only one who suffered from the underwater ordeal. The experience on the wreck and having to handle dead men, is the sort of thing most people find it hard to adjust to without some kind of practical or psychological support.

Nico's life was certainly impacted: 'It's better now. But I used to have quite a few nightmares about the corpses, and dreams of stepping on dead bodies…'

Nico didn't take a break, he kept diving — even right after saving Harrison, he was sent back underwater again. He believes that not stopping and thinking is perhaps the reason why he is still a diver. He still works at sea every day — and sails around in ships that are in many ways similar to *Jascon 4*, whose wreck has given him so many nightmares.

'Ever since then, even to this day, I'm never inside a ship without knowing exactly where I am and where my cabin is, and from my cabin — even if the vessel is upside down — I can find my way out the cabin. Knowing exactly where I am is always in the back of my mind. Another thing I usually check is if I can fit out through the window. And if there is something inside the cabin that I can smash the window with. Always.'

Nico and Harrison did not see each other after the accident. They had been in contact through social media and they both felt that the experience had bonded them in a way that was hard for people to understand who had not spent five hours together in life-threatening conditions inside a dark shipwreck. But Harrison lived in southern Nigeria, Nico was from Cape Town, South Africa, and was anyway out at sea half of the time. Although those places seem close to each other when you look at a map of Africa, it is not surprising that the two men never ran into each other, since more than 7,000 kilometres separate them. Their backgrounds are totally different. Harrison is from an extremely poor country and black. Nico is well-off and white. In their countries this made their friendship unlikely. But their shared experience gave them a bond for life.

Harrison remembers their first proper meeting: 'One day Nico came to see how I was doing. He saw the small, shuttered office I had ended up in and heard about the poor salary I was getting. Then he said, "Why don't you just take a diving job? It is quite well paid, and I can help you with a diving course." I said that diving was probably not for me, as I had become extremely afraid of water. Nico understood that well, but diving would be much better paid than what I was doing now, where I spent most of my salary on transport and accommodation since the shutter office was a long way from my own home and family. I actually transported myself through areas there that were dangerous and my everyday life in the stupid little shutter office therefore entailed a risk, because every week I had to go back and forth through them. Nico said that if I risked my life anyway to go to work, it might as well be for a much better job. And he thought he could help me to get a diving course.

'I said, "Hmm ... I'll think about it."'

Nico appreciated the strangeness of his idea: 'I know it was a weird suggestion I gave him. But the job he had just wasn't right — and it was like the only help I could think of. But I actually don't understand that he would seriously consider diving ... That someone who has experienced what he had, was actually willing to consider becoming a diver. It's quite strange. But he did.'

Harrison wasn't crazy about the idea at first: 'But I also didn't like my job in the small office ... So, Nico took me down to a diving school, close to where he lives and showed me everything and I could tell it was exciting and much better than the little office I otherwise wasted my life in.

'So, I made a decision that day. If Nico, who saved me and knows what I went through, still says, "You can become a diver if you want. You just need to get rid of your fear of water and take the diving course ..." If he says that ... then I can ... so, I started thinking about it. Why not go for a better job that might be more dangerous, but in return I would know that I risked my life for something good and made enough money to support my family? And I thought, "I have to get rid of my fear of water once and for all. So, I have to get used to the water again if I want to be able to get rid of that fear."'

Nico remembers the first steps: 'So, we met, and I helped him as much as I could. We started by just approaching the sea ... and looking at it.'

Harrison didn't find it easy: 'I started going down to the beach to sit near the water for a while. Later I could go into the water a little, just up to my knees, stay for a while and then come back up… Then I swam in the swimming pool. The first time I tried it went pretty bad… I couldn't, I was just so scared I swallowed water and bounced around and was afraid of passing out and when I got up, I was breathing really fast.'

Nico had his doubts: 'It took some time, and I wondered if maybe it was a bad idea after all… on the other hand, if he could overcome his fear of water, then he had fought the trauma and won. And in the end won very big if he ended up as a diver. So… there is a diving school in the town where I live in South Africa, and I managed to put Harrison in touch with the owner of the school.'

Harrison: 'Nico talked to the owner of the commercial diving course and the owner said if I really wanted to be a diver they should probably help me. I made the decision because Nico helped me… I started the diving course, and I overcame my fear of water and after some time I became a professional diver.'

Nico: 'So now he is a commercial diver, and he works regularly in the diving industry, and he is doing well. He's a pretty good diver.'

Harrison: 'Nico signed my first logbook. So, he was the first person to document that I was a real diver. And when I got my certificate, Nico picked me up and we went to his house. He took me around town before I left, and we became very good friends.'

But even though today Harrison has largely overcome his fear of water, there are of course some things, both good and bad, that will never completely disappear. One good side is that if he does ever experience a shipwreck again, there's a good chance that he will escape it better this time.

Harrison explains: 'Sometimes when I'm diving, I panic. It overpowers me quite slowly. But I've learned to get it off. I just think of something positive to be happy. Or I start singing. Sometimes when I dive and can feel the anxiety creeping in, I talk or sing to myself. But we have radio communication on, so when I sing, they think it's quite strange up on the diving ship, and they ask on the radio, "What the hell are you doing?" Then I answer, "I'm so happy because I'm going to do this diving job and I'm going to do the job so well that you'll give me your grandmother when I'm done." They'll laugh and we'll start joking. In this way, fear and panic disappear. But it's probably always in the back of your mind, waiting.'

Harrison during his diver training.

Tony: 'It's amazing that he's started to pursue a job as a professional diver ... with the way he started his underwater career, trapped sixty-two hours in an upside-down wreck with no diving equipment ... So ... It can only get easier from now on.'

14

Dancing Makes You Happy

The whole experience has made Nico look at many things differently: 'You realize how fragile life actually is. When someone is basically on the brink of death, and you manage to get them out of there and save their life — that same experience was horrifying and it was horrible to do ... all that stuff with the dead ... and then it was suddenly the most rewarding thing I've experienced when we found Harrison. The most rewarding thing ever in my life.'

Harrison sees fate's part in his future: 'I have a dream that I believe will one day come true. Of course, I hope that no-one will get hurt, but I believe that one day — just as I was saved — I will also save someone, now that I have become a diver.'

Nico: 'Experiencing the absolute joy of saving someone's life ... it was ... It's one of the best experiences ... I can only compare it to the birth of my children. There are few things that rival that feeling when you've done something to save someone's life.'

Harrison: 'The experience has given me something that is also good. My friendship with Nico. Nico has been my friend since the day after the incident. Although we are both at sea in different parts of the world, we keep in touch and see each other as often as possible. I think we are friends for life because we have shared an experience that no-one else can be a part of.'

Nico: 'The fact that Harrison survived and that he got a second chance ... and for me to be a part of that ... it's just ... his whole life is different now and he's using it to the fullest, so ... it's just a perfect ending to this experience.'

Harrison: 'The accident has changed the way I live, the way I think and the way I approach life. Actually ... before this ... Then I often got angry. I was sloppy with things. I always put myself in the centre ... wanted the whole world to myself. But when I saw my colleagues — with all their big dreams, families, and children — when I saw them disappear into the water and die, it changed my whole perception of life. So, I understand now that you have to do the right things at the right time. If you want to have a family, then you have to prioritize it. You must put your children before yourself. Make sure they have a future. Because you can't plan your way out of life. You never know what can happen. Things just happen sometimes. We dream about how life should be... but it is not certain that it will be like that. Today I don't take life so seriously. I never argue with anyone. I never get mad or angry. I have become a really calm person. When someone says something to me, my first reaction is to smile. I want to be a good person. I try to live like a newborn baby who knows nothing about life and what can happen. It just has to come. Just like the direction of the wind. It can change, and then you just have to adapt. Today I have small children and my whole life revolves around them. About being with them and making sure they have a good life. A life that is better than the one I have had. The experience on the wreck has completely changed me. To a better person. A much better person.'

Harrison sits, a smile across his face, in the little home-made film studio we have built in the heavily guarded accommodation in the middle of Lagos where we're living. We are interviewing him here while mercenaries stand guard outside the locked door. Harrison's voice has softened as we start talking about his children. I ask him what he does when he spends time with them.

'We're together... we do things together... we dance a lot. We can all really like that. It's great to dance. Dancing makes you happy...'

And he is right... it is difficult to argue with that.

We are about to finish the last of many interviews. As we start to pack up the equipment, Harrison puts on some of his favourite music and we play it through the speakers of the recording equipment. And then Harrison starts to dance. He dances just there, in our ugly homemade studio in front of a green screen background.

I can only agree with him, it does make you happy.

Harrison dancing in our DIY studio.

Postscript

The Open Hatch

The official explanation for the sinking of *Jascon 4* is that the captain of the tugboat sailed in rough weather with a cargo hatch open. Since it was therefore the crew's own fault that the ship sank, the families got very little compensation from the ship's owner.

However, we can see from the divers' video recordings that the hatch on the deck is not open. It is closed as it should be. So, it seems clear that the captain did *not* sail with that hatch open as the ship's owner claims.

Harrison says that the ship was tipped over at enormous speed and landed on the seabed within seconds, which is also backed up by the condition of the wreckage in the divers' video recordings. The ship smashed so far into the mud that it must have hit the seabed at some speed — with its bottom upwards. Sinking due to an open hatch would not happen like that. The ship would not roll over but land upright on the seabed, just as it had been on the surface.

The divers also found a thick towing cable at the bottom of the wreck. They could see — and film — that one entire side of the deck had been ripped open by the cable, which had obviously been pulled sideways across it.

When the accident happened, *Jascon 4* had just towed a large Russian oil tanker that was meant to fill up at one of the floating oil fields off the Nigerian coast. After a tow, the procedure is always for the tugboat to sail closer to the tanker, so that the tow line becomes slack. This allows the tanker crew to release the thick cable and sail away. While this is happening, it is extremely important that the oil tanker does not have its engine running because the towline can get caught in the propeller, pulling the tugboat sideways at great speed.

It is now so long after the events that it will be difficult to ever really be certain about what happened. But I have seen a photograph of the oil tanker's propellers entangled in a tow line, which other divers later had to remove. Under what circumstances this happened, unfortunately we do not know and it is probably best not to start drawing conclusions or casting innuendos without knowing the other side of the story. When Harrison started looking into it further, he was contacted by someone purporting to be a lawyer — there are doubts as to whether that was the case — who very strongly advised him not to talk about the matter. He says he has been threatened several times and advised to leave the country if he were to make an official charge. It is not certain Harrison would survive if he does this in Nigeria.

Our own research found that a Russian tanker was registered as being in a shipyard in Cape Town, at the time when it was actually filling with oil 7,000 miles away off the Nigerian coast. We also found out that the oil field the tanker filled from was 'not in use' at the time. It was closed. A tanker that size carries quite a bit of oil. As the barge was officially out of use at that time, the oil may possibly even have been acquired in an 'under the table' deal. If so, it would also not be surprising that they'd rather not be associated with this story.

We decided not to include the details of and accusations against the owners of the Russian ship in the documentary film on which this book is based. They would have been very difficult to prove, and it would probably have been dangerous for Harrison. The main part of the story, about Harrison's experiences in the wreck and the rescue operation, is hopefully exciting enough in itself. It does hurt a little not to be able to properly restore the reputation of the captain, tell the true story of the shipwreck and help the families of the crew of *Jascon 4* to get fair compensation. But that will have to wait for another film — at a later date.

The crew of *Jascon 4*

Captain
LOVEDAY KARIBO

Chief Engineer
Name unknown

Chief Mate
JOHNNY OHWONAM

Second Engineer
ODIDA MARTINS

Third Engineer
BASSY IDOLOR

Bosun
RICHARD EGBE

Able Seaman
MICHAEL EGDEDI

Able Seaman
RICHARD KUYOMA

Able Seaman
ONEYBEZE

Able Seaman
PETER AKERE

Cadet
LUCKY OLA

… and the Cook
OKENE HARRISON

How We Did It

It was no simple matter finding and interviewing the characters in this story. My poor, talented researcher — who can usually find me all sorts of strange people — toiled for weeks without finding the people who had actually experienced the wreck.

The diving industry is a sort of 'pirate' industry, where many people tell good stories, which, when you check them, usually turn out to differ quite a bit from the facts. Therefore there are also a whole lot of different versions of this story on the internet. But I think we dug deeper and got closer to the truth than anyone has ever managed to before, by speaking directly to the actual people involved and doing original research.

Even the stories told by Harrison and the divers contain errors. Over time, they have either remembered incorrectly, or have themselves been influenced by the incorrect information other people have got from the internet, so that they themselves are wrong now. But that is quite excusable, because none of them have had that full overview which comes from sitting for three years with all the recorded material and the detailed commentaries of everyone involved. There are almost one hundred hours of material from the divers' helmet cameras, where all communication — even when it is not said to the divers — is clear and distinct. Even Nico has not had the opportunity to hear all of it. It enables a remarkable knowledge of the details.

I interviewed nearly everyone involved many, many times and have hours of material which goes over the story again and again from every possible angle. Many of those involved have been incredibly helpful and most are naturally very proud to have helped save Harrison's life. However, it is a brutal reality that some people in South Africa grew up with values far from those we try to live by here in Europe. When I asked one potential interviewee if I could come down and speak to him about the rescue, his response was: 'Harrison? For me he's just another n***** from Nigeria.' So, we didn't think the interview would be worth the effort. But fortunately, there were plenty of very helpful people, plus great footage from the real operation. Here, I have to give huge thanks to offshore manager Tony Walker, who was a great help and stood by for the whole documentary production period. He spent enormous amounts time and effort helping me get everything right.

Nico's help was indispensable. His honest way of telling his story changed this from being just a tale about a brave rescue, into a story about actual, *real* people who, out of human compassion, acted as they would want others to act towards them. It has been an honour to get to know Nico and it is my hope that if one day I end up in a sinking ship, he will be somewhere not too far away.

Of course, meeting Harrison — after following his incredible experiences from such a distance — was a huge pleasure. But the fact that I got to meet such a warm and sympathetic person was a pleasant surprise. On documentary stories like this, you are not always so lucky as to find the main characters all incredibly likeable ... but the three main characters in this story — Tony, Nico and Harrison — were all extraordinarily nice, human and helpful men who, in my opinion, change this from an incredibly lucky rescue operation into a true story of a human miracle. Thanks for that, Tony, Nico, and Harrison.

In order to make the film, we also had to familiarize ourselves quite thoroughly with the construction of the sunken ship. There were only two photographs of the *Jascon 4* in existence. Offshore manager Tony Walker was kind enough to share the floor plans his team had been given when they had to rescue the drowned sailors. Through these we could build a model of the ship in 3D, get a feel for distances and create the underwater set needed to film reconstructions with actors, including of what Harrison was doing before Nico got to him. Skilled animators built a 3D model based on the plans of the ship and the real footage, so that we could show it sailing, capsizing and images of the wreck on the seabed.

We also built a life-size replica of Harrison's cabin, the corridors outside, a few extra cabins and a stairwell. We filled these with the inventory items we could see in the real footage, plus signs, handles and doors that were similar to the real ones. Then, of course, it all needed to be turned upside down. It was built it in such a way that the whole set could be lowered underwater, so we could film the sinking, the ship rolling violently upside down — with stuntmen in it — and not least, shots of Harrison in the flooded cabin when the ship was going down. None of which was filmed in reality, of course, as it happened more than two days before Nico got there with his helmet camera.

In the underwater set, we also shot footage of 'Nico' diving — seen from a distance — because on the real recordings nobody was filming what he was doing inside the wreck. This meant that with his help, we could reproduce Nico's actions.

Many experts helped with all this, but Tony Walker in particular was a huge help in making contact with everyone who had anything to do with the wreck and in getting hold of the original recordings from the divers' helmet cameras. I interviewed him several times in England, where he lives, on a sat vessel in Marseilles, France, as well as on his many visits to Denmark for follow-ups and to fact-check what I had gradually pieced together.

The one person I spent the most effort on has certainly been Harrison, because he was so hard to get hold of. The first of many interviews I did with him took place over Skype when he was offshore as a diver on a ship for months. When you do the work he does, you are at sea for six weeks at a time and do not come ashore. Furthermore, it was very difficult for me to go down to him where he was working, in Durban in South Africa, because this was right at the beginning of the Covid-19 outbreak and most borders and flights were closed. In the end, we worked out a way for me to travel down to him and agreed to meet in Nigeria when he came ashore at the end of his shift. We should have had six weeks while he was on leave, to make the first recordings. But when he finally got time off and should have come ashore, his employers decided it was cheaper for them not to go to a port, but to let everyone have their days off on board the ship. So, Harrison — much against his will — spent the next six weeks of free time at his workplace on board a big vessel somewhere in the middle of the ocean.

It was almost six months before it was finally possible to meet so we could film. We had given up on getting Harrison to Denmark or England, because I had by then experienced first-hand that trying to get a person into Europe from a country like Nigeria, is practically impossible. On the official side, there are visa requirements and rules that are really complicated and difficult to comply with, but it never dawned on me before that it would be *that* difficult. So, in the end the easiest thing was for us to travel to Nigeria and film Harrison there.

At the time there was a wave of unrest in Lagos, so everything was done with armed guards and accommodation in what looked more like a fortress with high walls, barbed wire and lots of armed men to look after us. We hung green screen fabric on the walls of one room in our heavily-guarded house to create a kind of interview studio, with the green background giving us the possibility to insert another background behind Harrison in the final film.

We hadn't taken into account that the electricity in Lagos goes out about once an hour, so the house's internal, very noisy, diesel generators had to be started to maintain power. It's quite annoying and I can't really recommend doing interviews in Lagos, as it's an extremely noisy city, which — at least while we were there — was also quite dangerous and difficult to live in. The last night our house was attacked by men with machine guns, with whom our guards got into a firefight. So, I would probably not suggest Lagos to anyone as a holiday destination. But the trip was worth it, because I spent some really exciting days with Harrison, with whom I became — and still am — very good friends. He explained his experiences to me in a very sympathetic and thoughtful manner. He is a very nice person. It's a good thing for the world that he didn't end his days inside that wreck.

Huge thanks (also from Harrison, I'm sure) to the brave men of the rescue team, who all made a fantastic, self-sacrificing effort for this unique operation to be carried out and succeed:

Saturation Diver
NICO VAN HEERDEN

Saturation Diver
JAIMIE BRENNAN

Saturation Diver
DARRYL OOSTHUIZEN

Saturation Diver
RICHARD BRECKLES

Saturation Diver
ANDRE ERASMUS

Offshore Construction Manager
JOE PUTTNAM

Saturation Diver
RICKY DRIJVER

Offshore Manager
TONY WALKER

Supervisor
COLBY WERRETT

Diving Supervisor
MIKE VALMAS

Diving Supervisor
STEPHAN OSSIEUR

Life Support Supervisor
ALISTER WILSON

Life Support Supervisor
JEAN PIERRE AL GARBY

Mechanical Dive Technician
CHRIS WATSON

Mechanical Dive Technician
PAUL WARDLEY

Electrical Dive Technician
DANIEL MALONE

Electrical Dive Technician
PAWEL TOMIAK

Life Support Technician
ALEX GIBBS

Life Support Technician
IVAN PARVANOFF

Lead Diver
DANIEL SISA

Lead Diver
MANUEL LEOTTE

Air Diver
MACHIEL DE LANGE

Air Diver
ANGUS TEMPLETON

Diver
NICK SHOOTER

Diver
JASON HENDRICX

Diver
WILL BLACKWELL

Acknowledgements

In addition to those that helped with the story, who I have already thanked, I would like to acknowledge those who worked with me on the documentary film, images from which appear in this book: producer Sofie Wanting Hadsing; additional camera Anushka Laubscher, Stefan Treshow, Mike Ekljaer and Reilly Kroch Marcussen; sound design Henrik Gugge Garnov/Gilyd; research Tony Walker and Luna Uhrskov Jacobsen; music George Keller; underwater reconstructions Workshop of Illusions; stand in Josef Nielsen; stunts Valdi Johannsson; saturation diver stand in Jens Erik Eriksen/SeaTek; safety diver Mike Ekljaer; underwater set and dive support Kim Alfasten/J.A. Shipping; animation EyeCandyFilm; VFX producer Linni Rita Gad; associate VFX producer Marko Antonov; VFX production assistant Mery Gobec; 3D artists Denis Bival, Gabriel Peicic, Matija Ternovec, Friso Tiesema and Sven Zinic; compositing artists Kelvin Chim and Lovro Kerdic; VFX technical directors Alekasandar Ribar and Davor Uidl; colour grading Kong Gulerod; produced by Been-There-Done-That-Production.

Lasse Spang Olsen
September 2024

Index

A
air pocket *20, 22-25, 79-80, 90-99, 147*

B
backup equipment *59*
bathroom *13-16*
bellman *45*
bends, the. See *diving: injuries: decompression illness (the bends)*
bodies *23, 41, 44, 67, 68-77, 144*
    recovery *44, 69-78*
bosun *14, 16*
bow *41, 72*
breathing *39, 79-80, 106-110*
bridge *17, 68*
buoyancy *138-140*

C
cabins *21, 26*
    captain's cabin *72*
    chief engineer's cabin *61*
    second engineer's cabin *19, 79*
cadet *25*
captain *17, 69, 151, 161-162, 163*
celebrations *142, 144*
    bitter sweet *144*
chief officer *17*
claustrophobia *87, 126*
commercial diving. See *diving: saturation diving*
compass *46*

compensation *151, 162*
control room. See *dive control*
corridors. See *passageways*
crabs *40, 80*
crampedness *43*
crayfish *40, 80*
creatures *40, 80*
crew *13-19, 24-25, 163*. See also *captain*
    cries for help *24*
    trapped *16*

D
dancing *158-159*
dangers *55-57, 60, 63-64, 114, 124, 132-133, 138*
darkness *16, 26-27, 39, 60, 115-116, 118*
decompression *33, 106, 109, 136, 144-145*
    compression chamber *30, 144-146*
disorientation *58*
distance from land *22*
dive control *29-36, 46-55, 57-64, 67-77, 83-88, 89-100, 101-110, 111-118, 119-140, 141-143*
diving. See also *harness; helmet; human physiology; lead vest; umbilical*
    injuries *23*
        decompression illness (the bends) *33, 59-60, 102, 136, 137, 144*
    saturation diving *30-37, 41-66, 56, 102, 107, 138*
    rules *44, 64*
    scuba diving *27-28, 59, 135*

diving bell *32, 41–42, 45, 46, 61, 133, 135–136, 139–140, 141–144*
diving cage *70–72*
doors *21, 47–52, 55–56, 58*
    construction *17*
    forcing open *49–52*
    locked *16–17, 47, 49–52, 76–77*
    unlocked *17*
dynamic positioning system *56–57*

E

emergency light *20–22, 25*
Erasmus, André *45, 61, 111–118, 123–124, 126, 139, 141–143, 147*

F

fear *40, 86, 87, 90, 92–94*
film studio/set *158–159, 166–168*
flashing. See *emergency light*
flotsam *55*
freediving *21–24*

G

gas expansion *22–23*
green rope *136–138*

H

harness *119*
Harrison. See *Okene, Harrison*
helium *45, 92, 107–109, 121, 145*
helmet *32, 45, 111–118, 119–120, 124, 126–127, 129, 132*
helplessness *24*
human physiology *107–109, 112*
hunger *25*

hypothermia *24–25*

I

interviews *165–168*

J

Jascon 4 *13–28, 46, 161–163*
    blueprints *48, 53, 84, 166*
    construction *13*
    hatch *161–162*
    photo *48*
    purpose *13*

L

Lagos *158, 168*
lead vest *138*
Lewek Toucan *29–37, 41*
lifeboats *17*
life jackets *20*
light *55, 92–93, 116.* See also *darkness; emergency light; torch light*

N

Nico. See *Van Heerden, Nico*
Nigerian waters *27, 34*
noise/sounds *18–19, 40, 92–93*

O

official explanation *151, 161*
offshore company *11*
oil barges *13*
oil industry *13, 161–162*
oil tankers *13*
    Russian tanker *161–162*

Okene, Harrison *13–28, 79–82, 89–99, 101–109, 111–118, 119–140, 141–148, 149–155, 157–159, 165–168*
   attempts to escape *16, 21, 23*
   bond with Nico *152–155, 157*
   car accident *149–151*
   disorientated *132, 141–143*
   dives *128–140*
   ear issues *149*
   faints *138–139*
   family *27, 80, 82, 103, 145, 147–148, 158*
   found by Nico *88, 89–91*
   growing up in Nigeria *27*
   health *106–110*
   impact *157–158*
   injuries *14, 40*
   job in office *151–153*
   learning to dive *153–155*
   swims for the surface *137–138*
   trapped again *150*
   trauma *149, 151–155*
   weakness *129, 137, 144*
Oosthuizen, Darryl *44–47, 49, 52, 54–55, 58, 60–61, 70–78, 83, 111–118, 121, 123–125, 130–131, 134–135, 139–140, 142–144, 147*
oxygen *25, 108*
   oxygen deprivation *39, 79–80, 92, 97, 106–110*

P

panic *63, 86–87, 125–129, 133–134, 139, 154*
passageways *16, 18–19, 21, 35, 54, 56, 72–73, 76, 83–84, 93, 102, 117*
pirates *16–17, 47*
praying *40*
pressure *22*

pressure chamber. See *decompression: compression chamber*

R

radio system *12, 32, 45–46, 58, 105, 119–120*
raft *26*
reconstructions *166–167*
rescue operation *123–140, 142*
rescue plan *102–110, 111–118*
rigor mortis *69, 71*

S

satellite positioning. See *dynamic positioning system*
shipwreck dynamics *55*
shipwreck penetration *43*
shock *75, 92*
shouting *19, 98*
sign language *97*
singing *81–82, 154*
sinking *14–28, 151, 161–162*
   speed *14, 161–162*
sledgehammer *50–52*
sound. See *noise/sounds*
sources *12*
speaking *97*
   high-pitched voice *92, 121, 142, 145*
stairs *84–87*
stern *72*
stress *64, 75, 103, 109*

T

thirst *25*
torch light *55, 59, 132*
towing cable *161–162*

trust *133*

U

umbilical *34, 41, 43–44, 54, 56, 58–64, 85–86, 111–115, 119, 123, 126, 130–131, 133, 138–139, 142*

V

Van Heerden, Nico *35, 41–65, 67–76, 83–88, 89–99, 102–109, 111–118, 119–140, 142–147, 152–155, 157, 166–167*
    bond with Harrison *152–155*
    emotional impact *69–72, 74–75, 86, 94, 96, 134, 157*
    energy levels *86*
    finds Harrison *89–91*
    gets stuck *62–64*
    trauma *152*
visibility *21, 45–46, 52, 55, 60–62, 67, 83–84, 86–87, 132*

W

Walker, Tony *12, 29–30, 35–37, 43–44, 52, 55, 74–75, 94–96, 102–110, 123, 125–126, 131, 133, 135, 137, 146, 155, 166–167, 167*
    emotional impact *74*
water ingress *17–19, 79*
water temperature *25*
weather *13*
Werrett, Colby *29*
wheelhouse *41, 47, 72*
wreck penetration *44*

DIVED UP
BOOKS FOR UNDERWATER EXPLORERS

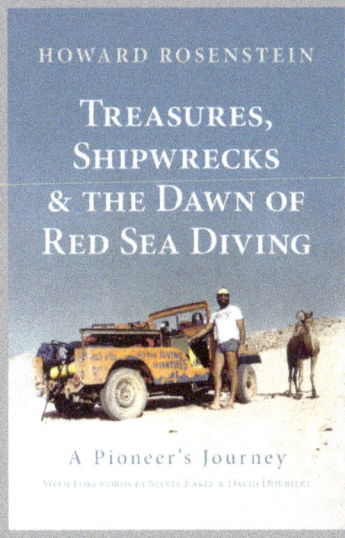
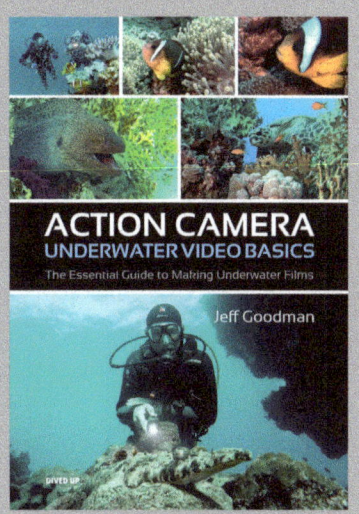
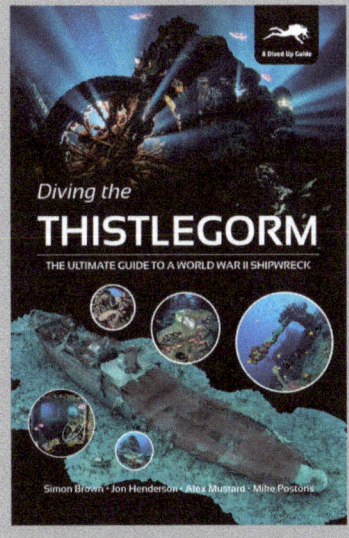
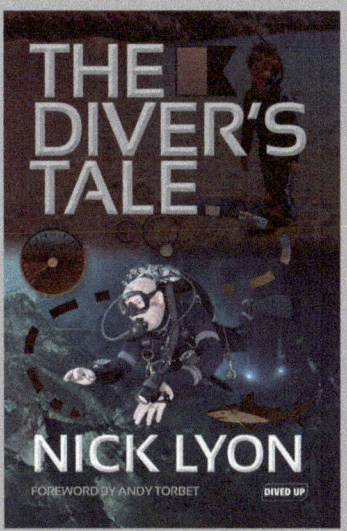

Discover the captivating world beneath the waves.

Explore a range of titles at www.DivedUp.com

www.ingramcontent.com/pod-product-compliance
Lightning Source LLC
Chambersburg PA
CBHW050929240426
43671CB00019B/2960